The PRIVILEGE

LESSONS FROM
THE HEART OF
A SHEPHERDESS

Kay SMITH

THE WORD
FOR TODAY

P.O. Box 8000, Costa Mesa, CA 92628 • Web Site: www.twft.com • E-mail: info@twft.com

The Privilege: Lessons from the Heart of a Shepherdess
by Kay Smith
Edited by Shannon Woodward

Published by The Word For Today
P.O. Box 8000, Costa Mesa, CA 92628
Web site: www.twft.com
E-mail: info@twft.com
(800) 272-WORD (9673)

Table of Contents

Foreword

I HAD BEEN a pastor's wife for two years—two lonely years—before I first had the chance to hear Kay Smith teach. As it happened, I heard her on the radio while in the drive-through line at a fast food restaurant. And I was in a bad mood.

Someone had said something horrible about my husband—a comment that was wholly undeserved, considering all the love and grace my husband had poured out on the one being so critical. Dave just laughed it off. "It's Philippians 3:10," he said. "This is the fellowship of His suffering."

But I could not laugh it off. I fumed as I replayed the comment, and conducted a vivid mental debate with that person, full of rebuke and pointy retorts.

And then ... I heard this voice on the radio. There was joy in that voice, and humor. I heard strength and conviction and determination. She began to talk about her husband and I heard her say "Chuck." A few sentences later, I heard "Calvary Chapel." I knew I had just found Kay Smith.

I listened while she told a story about a group of disgruntled people who had said horrible things about *her* husband … and how he had just laughed it off … and how she couldn't. She described her anger and indignation and frustration—all the things that were dwelling in me at that very moment. But then she began to share what God had spoken to her, and as she did so, the Holy Spirit pierced my heart. He told her—and me—that we were to love the people, even when they didn't love us back. We were to pray for them and look for ways to bless them. The Lord reminded us that this was the fellowship of His suffering.

I began to love Kay Smith in that moment. Her surprising honesty made me blink and sit up straight. Her refusal to pretty-up her own humanity made me trust her. And I found in her a mentor and a companion—someone who knew every pothole along my path and loved me enough to issue the travel warnings I needed.

Since that first radio teaching, I've been blessed to hear Kay speak in person a number of times at our annual pastors' wives' conferences. Even better, God made a way for me to know Kay personally. She is more delightful than I can describe here. She is more candid, more zesty, more lovely … more of everything you long for in a friend, and everything you need in a teacher. I've had the opportunity to sit with her for long talks, share meals, and walk the grounds of the Calvary Chapel Conference Center together under a warm Murrieta sky. I've asked her questions I can't ask anyone else and she has given me answers that are frank, and sometimes corrective, but always loving and encouraging. When Kay counsels you—whether in person, on the radio, or in the pages of this book—she gives you a little dash of "Look here, Missy" and a big dose of "I know you can do it." And we need both if we're to please God and bless the ones He's entrusted to us.

So often, in the midst of our conversations, I've found myself grieving for the young pastors' wives who missed the chance to sit under her teaching, and who have not had the opportunity to ask her their most fearful questions. For that reason, I am enormously grateful for the book you are holding in your hands. This is a collection of teachings Kay has given to pastors' wives over a span of twenty years' worth of conferences. More than that—it's a glimpse into her heart. Whether you are a pastor's wife, a ministry leader, a teacher or a mother, Kay has a soft spot for you. She knows how hard it can be to have others look to you for their needs. But she's also learned how to rely on God for the strength to tend them. And her great desire is to build you up in your faith so that you can tend your lambs as well.

I've selfishly come to think of Kay Smith as *my* Kay. If you know her, you likely feel the same way. And if you don't, let me say how delighted I am to introduce you to one of my most favorite people on the planet—a woman who is much younger than her years, transparent to a fault, and so filled with love for Jesus that it spills over onto all she encounters.

May you feel that love as you read Kay's words. And may you remember again what an awesome privilege it is to serve the living God.

Shannon Woodward
Editor
Senior Pastor's Wife
Calvary Chapel Marysville, WA

Introduction

I HAD ONLY been back with the Lord nine months when I met the man who would become my husband. I had just come out of college and dated a few of the boys I knew there, but I'd never met anyone before who compared with Chuck Smith.

On our first date, he talked about the sermon he was planning to teach in Santa Barbara that coming weekend. I fell for him right then and there. I listened to him and thought, *At last ... a godly man!* Neither of us really wanted to get married, and we made our feelings about that clear to each other on our second date. On our third date, Chuck asked me to marry him—and I did, just two months after we had met.

I think it's going to last. We celebrated our sixty-second anniversary this year. Which means that we've been in ministry together just as long, because Chuck took his first pastorate within weeks of our marriage. And let me tell you, I was woefully aware of my own inadequacy on that first day of my new position as wife of the pastor. I was excited, naturally, and curious about what was to come. But I didn't have any idea what I was supposed to *do* as a pastor's wife. I sure knew what they looked like though. They were kind of severe and they dressed just

right. And of course, their every movement was marvelous, perfect and godly. So I was a bit daunted, because I knew I didn't have any of that going for me. All I had was a little bravery.

Our first church was a small congregation in Prescott, Arizona. Chuck and I were barely twenty-one, and the first thing I noticed when we walked in that Sunday morning was that almost everyone in the room was over fifty. Before I could let that information really sink in, a lady walked up to me and said, "I am the adult Sunday school class teacher." Then she handed me her quarterly and added, "And now you are."

How's that for an introduction to ministry? I had never taught a Sunday school class in my life. I hadn't even read through the entire Bible. I'd only been back with the Lord for nine months … and married for only three weeks. I stood there wondering, *Oh my word, what does a pastor's wife do now?*

That was my first Sunday as a pastor's wife, and it was only the beginning of what has turned out to be a glorious journey. And I have to tell you, sixty-two years later, that God has never failed me once— not ever. I love telling you that, because I have a special place in my heart for pastors' wives and I know how hard this calling can be. I remember what it was like to be a young woman in the ministry, and I know now what it's like to be an older woman in ministry too. I know the paths you're on and the ones waiting for you around the corner, and it's a joy for me to have this chance to encourage you to keep walking. Sometimes the road can seem very hard and very long. But we've been given a tremendous privilege as pastors' wives—a privilege that most people never experience. Maybe you're in a rough place today. Maybe all you need is a reminder of the gift you've been given.

Several years ago, on one of our trips to Israel, a large group of us stood together in the field of Bethlehem. There happened to be a young Bedouin shepherdess there, tending to her flock of about fifty sheep. I found her completely fascinating, and I couldn't take my eyes off of her. Because she wore no veil, I could see her face very clearly, and from the position where I was standing, she couldn't tell that I was staring at her.

While I watched, I saw her bend down and pick up some rocks. I knew from previous trips and from listening to Chuck's sermons that shepherds sometimes use rocks to keep their sheep from running off. They'll throw the rocks just ahead of where the sheep is going, or they might even hit the sheep itself with a small rock to get its attention and to stop it from wandering off. But this shepherdess wasn't being gentle. When she threw those rocks, she threw them with a vengeance. She hated being out in that field, and it seemed she hated the sheep as well. In addition to her handful of rocks, she also had a big stick, and whenever a sheep was within her reach, she'd whack it as hard as she could, yelling and scowling. It was an awful thing to see.

From time to time, this woman would turn her eyes from the sheep to our group, and I could see the longing there. She wanted to be in any other place than where she was. For over an hour, I watched the emotions on her face—anger, fury, longing. I couldn't help but wonder, *Why is she here? Who sent her to this field?* I know a little bit about the Bedouin culture. Some men are good to their women, but many treat their wives and daughters worse than they would treat the animals they possess. I wondered if an angry father had sent this woman to the field. Or maybe she was sold into marriage at a young age, and her cruel husband forced her to tend the sheep. Whatever the case, it was clear she hated the work she had been sent to do.

Sometimes, beloved daughter, we find ourselves standing in a place we never asked to go, tending to a task we never wanted. And it's easy—if we keep our eyes cast down on the field and on the sheep—to yield ourselves to bitterness. Like the Bedouin shepherdess, we can get to the point where we scowl at the work we've been given, and dream of escape. Nevertheless, when we go the way of bitterness and regret and anger and longing, we misrepresent our heavenly Father and our Bridegroom. Instead of seeing the work He's given us as being an opportunity to bless and serve Him, we allow ourselves to despise the place where He's put us.

Have you felt this way in the past? Are you feeling this way right now? Maybe you're miserable in your marriage, and you don't think he's a good husband. Or maybe you don't think your husband is such a good preacher. I don't know where you are or what is going on in your life, but I do know that if you're angry about your calling or longing for another, you're missing the greatest opportunity of your life. You're missing the chance to influence others for Jesus.

You may not have asked for the role of pastor's wife. You may have never envisioned yourself having this position. But here you are. The question is, what are you going to do with this ministry God has entrusted to you? Will you rise to the calling, simply to bless and serve the Lord, and in so doing, influence an entire congregation toward Jesus? Or will you do the work begrudgingly, and misrepresent your Father to the people? Do you want to indulge in your bitterness and let others think that your Father is a cruel taskmaster? When you have a love for Jesus, people see that. When you lack love for God, they see that too. They know whether or not you love the Word, and they know whether or not you love your husband. And it makes a difference in their lives.

I've said many times that if I were to write a book for pastors' wives, I would tell you to do the following: love the Lord, love your husband, love your children, and love the people. Here is that book. Those are simple words, but they can be very difficult to do. If you'll let me, I'd like to share some of the mistakes I've made and some of the victories God has given me. We are walking this path together, and it is a journey of great privilege. I hope you will embrace your calling with a renewed sense of wonder—a renewed sense of "sent-ness." I want you to see that the Lord Jesus Christ sent you to that particular flock of sheep in your care. You've been called to come alongside that man who is doing his best to feed and tend them.

Just by virtue of being married to the shepherd, you are a shepherdess. You tend the flock just as he does. If you're not tending it, I really don't know how you're managing to avoid it, because if you stand in the church for any period of time, someone is going to approach you with a need. Don't you find that to be true?

In the beginning of our ministry, we used to love helping people so much that Chuck actually put an ad in the newspaper saying, "If you need counseling, come to us." It included our home phone number. I used to call people to ask, "How are you doing?" hoping they weren't doing well so I could then tell them how to live. I was twenty-two years old and had two years of psychology under my belt, and I thought I had all the answers. Now I think, *Oh Lord, unless You give it to me, I don't have answers for anybody.* But He is always faithful to provide what I need.

A while back, I received a call from a woman who had gone through a number of trials and failures—especially failures. In fact, her life was riddled with failures. She had been going to our church for a very long time, and I knew a lot about her life. And I was aware that the choices and decisions she made for herself were often very scary. We had talked and worked through issues and prayed together for years and years—but usually to no avail. Despite all my prayers, suggestions and counsel, she'd nearly always choose the worst of her options.

After another one of those phone calls, I thought, *I can't carry her any further. I just can't do it. So I'll tell her that I will pray for her, but I can't keep ministering as I am now.* My life had become much busier and I had more responsibilities than ever. Besides, I wasn't seeing any fruit from our conversations. So I turned her over to a good friend of mine at the church. For almost two years, my friend did a good job ministering to this woman. But then I received the phone call. She said, "Guess what?" and proceeded to tell me about yet another failure.

I will admit to you that my immediate thought was, *This is it. I'm all done with this nonsense and now I'm going to straighten her out.* Have you ever had that feeling? When you've carried someone for ten years and they don't seek the Lord, they don't obey the Word, they don't listen to your counsel, and they just continue to do the same things over and over, you sometimes feel like giving up. In my flesh, I wanted to say, "This is it! Quit doing what you're doing!"

So I tried. I responded, "I want to tell you something ..."

That's all I got out, because she started talking again. She blurted out her newest story all in a rush, and then she said, "I cannot believe this has happened to me!"

And as she was saying those words—"I cannot believe this has happened to me"—God intercepted. All of a sudden, He overrode my flesh and put such a love in my heart for her that I began to prophesy to this woman. With no help from me at all, He caused His words to begin flowing through me to her. I said, "The Lord loves you. He loves you with an everlasting love. He understands your pain. He understands your failures." All I could do was speak His love to her.

After at least two precious minutes of that, I stopped. And on the other end of the phone, the woman sobbed. She sobbed and sobbed and sobbed. It was as if the poisons of a lifetime were being poured out. Suddenly, she began to see that God understood the origins of her thoughts. He understood all the ugliness in her childhood. He knew why she had made the decisions she had made. And He loved her still.

I wanted to share that with you, beloved daughter, because it applies to you as well. God sees and understands. He knows why we do the things we do. He knows our failures and He loves us in spite of them. God loves you tremendously. And He's not scoring you on the job you're doing as a pastor's wife. I really want you to hear that. Your willingness to serve others on His behalf is a good way to demonstrate your love for Him, but it isn't a way to earn His love. You already have that—and you have it in abundance.

Paul's prayer for the Ephesians was that,

> Being rooted and grounded in love, that they may be able to comprehend with all the saints what is the width and length and depth and height of God's love (Ephesians 3:17-18).

That's my prayer for you too. I pray that you will begin to comprehend just how much God loves you, because when we begin to gain a greater sense of that love, our own love for others begins to grow by leaps and bounds. When we know we're loved, something precious happens.

We're released from "self." We're built up and encouraged, and we stop focusing on our own lives and start looking for ways to bless others.

Years ago, Hannah Hurnard wrote a beautiful book called *Hinds' Feet on High Places* which tells of the allegorical journey taken by a girl named Much-Afraid. Like Hannah, Much-Afraid had a crooked mouth and crippled feet. In the book, she writes this little song:

> "I am not fair save to the King,
> Though fair my royal dress.
> His kingly grace is lavished on
> My need and worthlessness.
> My blemishes he will not see
> But loves the beauty that shall be." [1]

That's exactly what God loves in you. He sees you as you're going to be at the end of this journey—perfected in Him.

Father, Your Word tells us in 1 Timothy 1:12 that we are in the ministry because You have enabled us, and counted us faithful, and placed us right where You wanted us to be. Oh, renew the wonder of those words to us! May You give each one of us fresh eyes for the privilege, and tenderize our hearts to love again, and teach us to tend Your lambs faithfully—to the praise and the glory of Your name.

We ask it in Jesus' name. Amen.

Chapter One

A RIGHT
RELATIONSHIP

FOR THE longest time, I didn't like to be called "the pastor's wife," because whenever I heard those two words spoken together, an image sprang into my mind of the perfect woman—the woman who fit this role. She always did the right thing. She always said the right thing. She behaved properly in every circumstance … and she wasn't me.

Well, sixty-two years have passed since that title was first conferred on me, and in some ways I guess I still have a rather negative image of those two words. I'm Chuck Smith's wife and I like being known as Chuck Smith's wife. I like that much better than being known as a pastor's wife, and yet I want to live up to everything that those two words mean—everything that I ought to be.

The Privilege

Over the years, as I've wrestled with my role and asked God to open my eyes to all that it means, He has taught me one simple truth: if I spend my life living to please Him, I will spend my life well. I will fulfill my role as a wife, mother, friend—and pastor's wife—if I will just keep that one goal in mind.

When Chuck spoke on Ezekiel 9:8, he focused on three words: "I was left." In those three words he brought out an important fact. If you're alive today, it's because God has left you on the earth for a divine purpose. There's something He wants you to accomplish. Otherwise, He would have already taken you home. It's a comfort to me to know that my time is in His hands, and I will remain alive until He has accomplished in me all He desires to accomplish. Doesn't that comfort you? A lot of us have had experiences where we could have died.

I remember one summer when Chuck and I were in England for a convention. We had just left our hotel and we were standing together on the sidewalk with a friend of ours, and I started to walk across the street. I was in a very happy mood, and to be honest, I was more attuned to the song I was singing in my heart to the Lord than I was to the traffic. Also, it didn't help that I was in England, where the correct thing to do is to look right instead of left. But I wasn't thinking about that. In the state of mind I was in, I did what we do at home in America: I looked left instead of right. Not seeing any traffic coming, I stepped onto the road so far in front of Chuck that he could not reach me. I didn't see the car barreling towards me until he screamed, "Kay!" It was the most frantic I had ever heard his voice in all our years of marriage, and the sound of it made me jump back. By doing that, the car missed me by inches. I could feel it as it zoomed past me. It really was a miracle of the Lord. When Chuck and our friend came out of their frozen state, we all began to praise God for saving my life.

That experience brought home the awareness that I'm on this earth for a divine purpose. It made me decide that whatever God wants me to do, I want to do. I want to fulfill that purpose—that role—for which I'm here. And maybe you don't like the word "role." Well, I wish I had another word for you, but I don't. We've each come to this position from a different background. Some of us were raised in Christian homes and found ourselves in church every Sunday morning and Sunday night, and perhaps every other night of the week as well. Some though were not raised in a Christian home. For those people, their idea of Sundays is quite different. It's a day to rest or to have fun. Some of you did not marry a pastor initially. Your husbands were businessmen or construction workers or something else before God called them into the ministry. That can be quite an adjustment.

My heart goes out to those of you who fell into this role with a thud. You woke up one morning and thought, *What in the world am I doing as a pastor's wife?* I wish for you women in particular that there was some sort of pastors' wives' manual. It wouldn't be so much a manual of do's and don'ts as it would be a manual of how to's. "Here's how you handle this disaster and here's how you counsel for this situation …" The Bible does not have anything to say about pastors' wives, does it? It doesn't tell us where to begin in this role we've been given. Since it doesn't, the best thing I can tell you is to begin with your relationship with the Lord.

Unless your relationship with the Lord is right, nothing else in your life will be right—and that includes the ministry. If the vertical isn't right, the horizontal never will be. What does it mean to have a right relationship with the Lord? First of all, it means loving God with all your heart, soul, mind and strength. It means walking in unbroken fellowship with Him. It means acknowledging Him in all your ways.

It means walking in obedience to His Word—and if you don't obey, it means confessing and repenting immediately for your disobedience.

It's interesting that one of the definitions in *Webster's Dictionary* for the word "spiritual" comes from the Latin word "breathing." [2] So if we're asking the question, "How do I maintain my spiritual life?" we may as well ask, "How do I keep breathing?" How do I keep alive in Jesus? On those dark, dreary, foggy days, how do I keep that fire burning within my soul? How do I rise above my feelings and minister effectively? When someone calls me on those dark, cloudy days and tells me, "Hey, I'm thinking of getting a divorce," sometimes I think, *Good idea. Do it.* Have you ever felt like saying that? We need to keep that breath of God coming through us so even on the dark days, the power of God will work in us to minister in a way which pleases Him and enables us to give the hopeful answers that people need.

The secret of staying in a right relationship with God begins with looking at Him first thing every morning. Years ago I heard someone at a pastors' conference say, "Never think your people are more spiritual than they are." I would like to believe that every pastor's wife has a devotional life. But it's doubtful. The truth is, a great many pastors' wives do not spend time every day reading God's Word and praying. You simply can't survive in the ministry without a consistent devotional life. And you certainly can't carry out the will of God as you should.

There's something very special about seeking God in the early morning. I love what David said in Psalm 5:3:

> In the morning, O Lord, you hear my voice; in the morning I lay my requests before you and wait in expectation (*NIV*).

What is David really saying? "God, I need something from You for this day. This morning, I direct my prayer to You and I look to receive from You what I need for this path. Lord, I don't know what's ahead of me—but You do."

The Amplified Bible says,

> In the morning You hear my voice, O Lord; in the morning I prepare a prayer, a sacrifice for You and watch and wait for You to speak to my heart.

Do you watch and wait in the morning for God to speak to your heart? Or do you get up and just start through the day lickety-split?

You might read that and think, *First thing in the morning? My house is a disaster first thing in the morning. There's breakfast to fix ... and lunch ... and kids to send off to school ... and diapers to change. There's no way I can sit quietly before the Lord first thing in the morning.* I agree. You can't possibly do it ... unless you can get up half an hour earlier. Or unless you ask God to show you a time when you can stop and meet with Him. It is up to you to make the determined resolution to keep the morning watch with Him. He'll arrange the time and the opportunity. You just need to have the willing heart.

Now, we all have days when we miss that morning watch. You have an early meeting, or maybe you've overslept. It's happened to me too. But I have found ways to meet with God even when I'm running out the door. I might pull some promises out of my promise box and read those throughout the morning. Or I'll ask God to bring a Scripture to meditate upon. He never fails to do that. I'll sing a hymn or praise Him in other tongues. Back when I was nursing my babies, I'd put my baby on one side of me and my Bible on the other. Those were precious times. It was so much better to fill up on God's Word than to turn on the TV and fill up on junk.

The key is to be persistent. Write verses on index cards and tape them near the kitchen sink so you can read them while you're washing dishes. Hang up plaques with Bible verses on them. A nice benefit to this— your kids will grow up memorizing those verses too.

Some would read that and think, *That's just so legalistic.* Maybe because of your temperament, you don't have a natural bent toward having a daily quiet time with the Lord. Just because you don't want to do it doesn't mean you don't need it desperately. Ask God to move you beyond your temperament.

Job said, "I have treasured the words of His mouth more than my necessary food" (Job 23:12). We women think about food a lot. If we're not cooking it to feed others, we're avoiding it in order to lose a few pounds. But here Job is declaring that the words from God's mouth are more important than his necessary food. It didn't matter to Job to feed his body as much as it mattered to take in God's Word to feed his spirit. I want that to be true of you as well. You know, if Job hadn't hidden God's Word in his heart, he wouldn't have been able to endure his trials. And he certainly wouldn't have been able to say, "Though He slay me, yet will I trust Him" (Job 13:15). I doubt he would have trusted God at all. It takes great trust in God to continue living day after day when it would be far easier to end your own life. But because Job treasured God's Word in his heart, he trusted Him.

If Satan can convince you that it's legalistic to have a daily quiet time, he'll be able to deaden you spiritually. If we don't get our food from God, we'll get it from His enemy. Satan is the prince of this sin-cursed world we live in, and he uses every possible device to speak to you—

your friends, the media, self-help books—it doesn't matter to him. The only way we can fight his whispers is to set ourselves at the feet of Jesus. It's there we are strengthened and equipped to triumph over the enemy.

When we've been with Jesus, His Holy Spirit gives us discernment about the wrong thoughts that pop into our minds. He'll say, "That thought is of the flesh," or "That's of Satan." He helps you to discern that which God is speaking to you and that which the enemy is whispering to you.

It is amazing how many ungodly thoughts Satan will try to plant in our minds. But we who belong to God have His Holy Spirit within us to do battle for us against those thoughts. Your daily quiet time will draw you closer and closer to Him so that when those thoughts come in, you will have discernment.

If Satan can't deceive you that a daily quiet time is legalistic, he'll try to deceive you that it's dull or pointless. You can tell he's deceiving you if you say, "I just don't have a desire for a quiet time," or "I don't get anything out of it." Listen, as a pastor's wife, you need to meet with Jesus daily. You have to. People will bring you their heartaches and their problems. If you don't feed your spirit daily, what will you give them? I'll tell you what you will give: your flesh. And God forbid you should ever give people counsel out of your flesh. We are not to play God in people's lives. Do you realize the destruction you can cause in a life or in a family if you try to counsel out of your own fleshly wisdom? You can destroy someone's marriage that way.

Every time someone comes to me with a heavy problem, I see that person as being sent by God. I pray, "God, guard my lips." I would much rather give a person no answer at all than to give an answer that's not from the Lord. It doesn't bother me to say, "You know, I don't have an answer from the Lord for you. Let's pray." Don't be afraid of saying, "I don't know." Be afraid to counsel out of your flesh.

Then there's you. If you don't meet with God daily, where else will you find the strength for your own problems? Where does a pastor's wife go for help? What if your husband is behaving in a way that you just can't stand? I would love to think that every pastor and his wife are delighted with one another, but the fact is, there can be strife. If that's the case, where do you turn? You have to go to the Lord.

For probably the first five to ten years of my marriage, I was a secret complainer. I didn't do it around other people, but at home I was a griper. I didn't like this and I didn't like that … and you know, complaining is never effective. It's only when I took my heartaches to the Lord that anything good happened. Gradually, the Lord worked in me and He worked in Chuck. That's how He does it. Today I have the marriage I've always wanted. I enjoy Chuck so much and we are closer than we've ever been.

Chuck never liked to write me little notes or letters. In fact, he hated that sort of thing, which was one of my biggest complaints. I wanted more approval and more appreciation and more of this and more of that. You know, gripe, gripe, gripe. But then one day he wrote me the dearest note. I'd been away at a retreat and when I got home I found it tucked under the covers of our bed. He was downstairs in the study at the time, so I sat on the bed and read his note—and sobbed and sobbed. I called him on the phone in his study and when he answered, I said, "There's a stranger in the house and I have fallen madly in love with him and I hope he never goes away." It was so precious. So don't be discouraged in your marriage, but rather realize the only thing that will hold you fast through the dark days is the counsel and wisdom you receive from the Lord.

You know, the world thinks nothing ever goes wrong in pastors' homes. Do you realize that? But our homes, of course, are just like everyone else's. We have pipes that burst, washing machines that overflow, and stacks of dirty clothes waiting to be washed. Sometimes we get the Monday morning blues just like other people. Our husbands can be difficult. Our children can be impossible, or get bad grades, or run with a bad crowd. All these things are just as painful and as wearisome to us as they are to anyone else who experiences them. You need to know what to do. Daily you need to have this quiet time alone with the Lord.

You were born to have fellowship with God. You are meant to enjoy your relationship with Him and to live in a continual awareness of His presence with you. God wants you to sense His constant presence with you every hour of the day, whether you're awake or asleep. You can't hide from God's presence, but you can lose your awareness of Him. I've been at my absolute worst when I have lost my consciousness of His presence. Yet when I'm aware of His nearness, I'm calm and quiet in spirit.

The term "daily devotion" can cause some to cringe. They see themselves forced to their knees for hours on end, getting nothing out of it. The same is true for "quiet time." People sometimes equate that with boredom. They can't imagine anything exciting happening during a thing called "quiet time." Of course, nothing could be further from the truth. How can meeting with God—the Creator of the universe and everything in it—be dull? If that's been your thought, ask God to give you a brand new picture in your mind. Whenever I think of the word "devotions," I see Mary sitting at the feet of Jesus, loving Him and listening to His every word. Every so often I like to reread Luke 10:39-42, just because I need to be reminded that Jesus wants me to be a Mary.

Maybe "quiet time" is not so much an issue of cringing as it is an issue of confusion. If you're new to the ministry—or maybe a woman who is new to the faith—it's quite possible that you have simply never been taught the basic steps to having a devotional life. So now that we've discussed the "why's" to have a devotional life, I want to give you some "how's." Before we can serve the Lord, we must first be devoted to Him. Devotion always comes before service. Even if you're a woman who has been walking with the Lord for a very long time, it doesn't hurt to go over these basics again.

The first step to having a devotional life is making a commitment to read your Bible every day. Every day. Whatever else happens, you must put God's Word before your eyes *every single day*. Now, in reality, we don't always manage to do it. But let's agree together that we should do it and that we need to do it, right? Be in God's Word every day.

When you need to be assured on this point, read Joshua 1:8.

> This Book of the Law shall not depart from your mouth, but you shall meditate in it day and night, that you may observe to do according to all that is written in it. For then you will make your way prosperous, and then you will have good success.

The book of Joshua is a favorite of mine because I love the instructions God gives to him. You can't get any clearer instruction on the importance of meditating on Scripture than what you read in Joshua 1:8. Read it often. Memorize it. And most importantly, do what it says.

The word "meditate" means to do more than just read. It's possible to read something and completely forget what it says the very next minute. But when you meditate on what you've read, you actually think about it. You think about it when it's in front of you, and you think about it when you're away from it. You apply it to yourself. *What does it mean to me personally? How does this apply to my life?* If you don't understand what you've read, search it out. Read a commentary or two. Check other translations. Or go to the pastor and ask him. You have pretty close access to him, so you can do that.

When we first started out in the ministry, I didn't know much about the Bible. I knew the Bible stories because I had gone to Sunday school, but I knew absolutely nothing about the Pauline epistles. I couldn't have taught a kindergartner—I really couldn't. I was terrified. I thought, *What if somebody asks me a question and I can't answer it?* I didn't know what to do. So I decided I'd better start studying.

Well, I sat down and began reading, but I was still so new in the Lord, I couldn't understand the passage. I remember stopping at Genesis 3:15 and thinking, *What in the world does this mean? I will put enmity ... what is enmity? ... between the serpent ... the serpent? What's that supposed to mean?* That's how ignorant I was of the Word of God. So I asked Chuck what I should do. He told me to get a *Halley's Bible Handbook*, so that's what I did.

For five years I brought my *Halley's Bible Handbook* to church every single Sunday, because I never knew if someone might approach me after the service to ask me a question. "Kay, I was reading in Jeremiah this week and I got to this verse ... do you know why God said that?" Right in front of the person, I'd open my *Halley's* to find an answer for them. I'd say, "You know, I'm still kind of new too, so let's find out together." *Halley's* should give me a commission—they really should. I can't even guess at how many people I've urged over the years to buy themselves a *Halley's*. It's the best and the simplest Bible handbook that anyone could have.

I will admit that I didn't have—or want—a devotional life at that particular time. But I knew I needed to saturate myself in the Scriptures if I wanted to survive as a pastor's wife. And because I knew that Chuck's mom read ten chapters out of the Old Testament every morning and five out of the New Testament every night, I figured I'd better start with at least five chapters a day. But I became so intent on reading those five chapters a day that I didn't care about the meaning of what I was reading, nor did I listen for God to speak to me. I just whisked through my chapters and got them out of the way. If you had asked me that night what I had read in the morning, I could tell you the book and the chapter, but I couldn't remember a single truth that I had read from those chapters. I didn't grow through it, I didn't learn through it, and I know now I didn't please the heart of God.

Then I read a book about George Muller and how he would read the Bible each morning until it spoke to him. As soon as that happened, George would stop and meditate on that verse or passage for the rest of the day. I began to do that, and I still do it to this day. I find the exact Scripture I need. God will lead me to the right passage because He knew I would need to meditate on that truth for something that would come up in my day.

Note that Joshua 1:8 doesn't say we are to meditate once a week. It says "meditate in it day and night." Even on those days when we've already been to church? Yes, even on those days. And why are we to do it? "That you may observe to do according to all that is written in it. For then you will make your way prosperous, and then you will have good success."

This verse promises if we will meditate on God's Word, we will be able to obey it. Then this will lead to success. It won't be success in the eyes of the world, necessarily, but it will be eternal and everlasting success in God's eyes. And that's the only kind of success that matters.

Sometimes a woman will have the attitude, "I'm in church on Wednesday night and twice on Sundays, and that's enough." No, it's not enough. God has not called you to a part-time relationship. He's called you to a daily relationship. What if you just saw your husband on Wednesday nights and Sundays? What kind of a marriage would that be? What kind of a relationship would you have? If you want to have a strong and right relationship with the Lord, then you need to meet with Him every day.

Psalm 1:3 tells us that when we absorb God's Word into our spiritual bloodstream, we will be "like a tree planted by the rivers of water, that brings forth its fruit in its season." Let it be absorbed. Can you remember at dinnertime what you read in the morning? Check up on yourself. Pay attention to how well you're retaining what you've read.

Then, after you read, take time to pray. Now, some days you will have lots of time for prayer, and other days you won't. But it's so important to stop and commune with the Lord no matter how much time you have. Talk to Him. If you need to repent of anything, repent and ask for cleansing. Then ask for direction for your life, and intercede on behalf of others. Cast your cares on Him. Ask Him to fill you with more and more love—for Him, for your husband, for your children, and for your congregation. Then, after you've talked to God, spend some time listening, because He wants to speak to you too. He wants to answer your questions for the day, and He wants to impart His attitudes, His compassion, His strength and His desires to you. Begin a journal to write down your prayer requests, the answers you receive to those prayers, and anything you hear from God during your time of quiet communion.

As to your posture when you pray, it's really not important whether you sit or kneel. But I will tell you when I'm deeply burdened in prayer, I drop to my knees. Sometimes I am literally on my face before the Lord. I had two prayer buddies in the church ... and let me say here that I hope you have prayer buddies too. If you don't, ask God to provide them for you. At times we had been so burdened for some of the needs at Calvary Chapel or for our own needs that we would begin our prayer in a chair and we would end up praying on our knees or even flat out on our faces. I'm not instructing you to do this, but I am saying that there are many different postures in prayer, and you want to keep yourself open to them all.

The most important thing is that you spend time in prayer. However you do it, lift your heart to the Lord and commune with Him. It's been said that we kneel weak, we rise in power. Don't you love that? And the Puritan poet, William Cowper, had this to say about prayer: "Satan trembles when he sees the weakest Christian saint upon his knees." [3] Doesn't that make you want to pray more and more? Whatever it takes, and whatever position you assume, make sure you take the time to pray.

And then, be filled with the Spirit. Sometimes people think, *I received the Holy Spirit when I was born again, and that's all I need.* You did receive the Holy Spirit when you were born again, but you need to be filled to overflowing. As Chuck so often asks, "Is the Spirit gushing out of your life in torrents?" In speaking of the one who believes in Him, Jesus said, "From his innermost being will flow rivers of living water" (John 7:38 *NASB*). It's the living water flowing out of your life that touches other lives. Adorable personalities, beautiful faces, and perfect clothes aren't enough. Time spent with Jesus and a constant filling of His Holy Spirit are needed if you're to touch other people. So before you leave that time of fellowship with the Lord, ask the Holy Spirit to fill you anew—and then ask Him to spill out of you onto everyone you meet that day.

I cannot stress strongly enough your need for daily devotions. Having a quiet time will keep you in a right relationship with God—and that will keep you in a right relationship with your husband, your children, and your congregation. Making a commitment to seek God every day does not put you under bondage—it brings you the greatest freedom you can know in Christ Jesus. This is the secret to an ever-deepening relationship with your Lord and Savior.

Chapter Two

WATCHMAN ON THE WALL

I RARELY EVER cry at funerals. That's because most of the time, I know the person who died is with the Lord. And if they aren't, crying is not going to help at that point. So I just don't. I see the service as an opportunity for Chuck to preach a salvation message to reach those who do not yet know the Lord. And though I love the people who are grieving and my heart grieves with them, I don't usually do it with tears.

But years ago, while sitting in the funeral service for a friend from church, I began to sob. I sobbed and sobbed and sobbed. People were looking at me and someone said, "My, Kay loved Tanya so much."

I did love Tanya Corwin. She and her husband, Herb, had been with us since the first year we came to Calvary Chapel. She was a dear friend whom I loved deeply. But that wasn't why I was crying. I cried because the body of Christ had just lost an intercessor.

I would turn to Tanya when the heavy prayer requests came in. I'd call her and say, "Tanya, agree with me on this, will you?"

She'd always answer, "Not only will I agree with you, but let's pray right now ... and I'll keep praying until I hear back from you that everything is okay." She was that person for me all through the years. I depended on her. Now she was gone, and I didn't know who would be able to replace her.

I cried like my heart would break. I sobbed all through the sermon and throughout the entire memorial service. I just couldn't stop. Afterwards, walking quickly through the foyer, I thought, *Lord, please get me to the car before anybody says anything.* But a friend stopped me and held me. "Kay, I have never seen you cry like this. What is the matter with you?"

That started me going again. I burst into tears, threw my arms around her and said, "The intercessor's gone! The intercessor's gone. Who will take her place?"

But do you know what God did? He raised up a Monday morning prayer meeting full of intercessors—women who carried the torch of prayer. Instead of just one chief intercessor, God supplied a whole group of them. And then God raised up all-night prayer meetings, and twenty-four-hour prayer groups—people who faithfully prayed around the clock.

Every church needs intercessors—people who know how to take hold of the horns of the altar and intercede between God and the people. Without those intercessors, your church will never become all that

God intends. That's because God shapes the world through prayer. He empowers the church through prayer. He heals the brokenhearted, breaks addictions, and opens deaf ears, all through prayer. Do you want to reach the lost? Do you want your church to be empowered to minister effectively? Then you need to pray, and you need to get your women praying. It begins with you. You have to be the one to start it. Prayer is the most powerful ministry you can have in your church—and one of the easiest ministries to neglect. And that breaks my heart.

If I could inspire you to do just one thing, I would inspire you to pray. In fact, I am begging and beseeching you to become a woman of prayer. Perhaps you already do pray, but I'm asking you to go even deeper. Become a woman of prayer such as you've never been before. Our world needs it and the church needs it. Not only does the church need your prayers, the church has a right to those prayers. They deserve a pastor's wife who prays for them. Do you know that? You owe them that. A prayerless pastor's wife is a menace to the church. She's a menace. But a pastor's wife who prays? She is a gift and a blessing to the body of Christ. She is a watchman on the wall.

God's Word is full of exhortations about prayer. First Thessalonians 5:17 instructs us to, "Pray without ceasing." James 5:16 reads,

> Confess your trespasses to one another, and pray for one another, that you may be healed. The effective, fervent prayer of a righteous man avails much.

Paul speaks about our responsibility to intercede for one another in Ephesians 6:18:

> Praying always with all prayer and supplication in the Spirit, being watchful to this end with all perseverance and supplication for all the saints.

The Privilege

In *The Amplified Bible*, this verse says,

> Pray at all times (on every occasion, in every season) in the Spirit, with all manner of prayer and entreaty. To that end keep alert and watch with strong purpose and perseverance, interceding in behalf of all the saints (God's consecrated people).

And then there's Philippians 4:6-7,

> Be anxious for nothing, but in everything by prayer and supplication, with thanksgiving, let your requests be made known to God; and the peace of God, which surpasses all understanding, will guard your hearts and minds through Christ Jesus.

In other words, Paul exhorts us to pray at all times, on every occasion, every chance we get, wherever we go, no matter what happens—and when we do that, peace will be ours.

This passage is so familiar to most of us that it's easy for the words to go past our eyes without ever making their way to our hearts. But I remember one time when the Lord highlighted that passage to me in a way I couldn't ignore—just when I needed it most.

When my daughter, Cheryl, was just three weeks old, we moved into a parsonage in the courtyard of the church Chuck pastored in Chino, California. This new church was so much bigger than our last church that the phone rang constantly—all day long. I had three other kids too—Janette, Chuck Jr. and Jeff—and I was very, very busy. I was nursing a baby plus doing all the cooking, cleaning and laundry for six people. We had no dryer, and back then there was no such thing as disposable diapers. So I was washing and hanging mountains of diapers. To this day, I can remember how incredibly busy my life was then.

One day I received a call ... and it was just one call too many. You know that feeling? I had spent an hour-and-a-half ministering to the woman who had called—an hour-and-a-half I didn't have to spare. Even before the call, I had already felt overwhelmed. I needed to hang the diapers on the line, pick up the kids from school, look over the church books, and then think about dinner.

On top of that, somebody was coming by later that night to talk to Chuck, which meant vacuuming the house. As I pushed the vacuum around Chuck's desk, the tears poured down my cheeks. I said, "Lord, I can't go on. I really can't. I'm through, Lord. I'm through." But then, just as I was thinking that the only thing left to do was run, I glanced down at the top of Chuck's desk. There lay a Christian magazine opened to the last article. In big, bold letters I saw the verse from Philippians 4:6-7.

> Be anxious for nothing, but in everything by prayer and supplication, with thanksgiving, let your requests be made known to God ...

I read it a second time, and then a third. Suddenly it dawned on me. I should be asking God to take care of this whole situation. I thought, *I'm His child ... I'm in His hands. All I need to do is pray.* So I turned off the vacuum and prayed, "Lord, I'm not going to move one more step until I feel Your peace flood over me."

He gave me peace for that day, and then the next. Day after day, as I meditated on this verse God had given me, I received peace from Him. And you know, it even seemed like He lengthened the days for me. I found I was able to get more done. The funny thing is that the magazine article was entitled, "How to Avoid a Nervous Breakdown." God is faithful, isn't He?

Prayer changes everything. It is the vehicle through which God works. So why don't we pray more? There's no good answer for that. A big part of the problem is that we're self-indulgent. We'd rather be out shopping or visiting with our friends. We'd rather watch TV than get on our knees. I've heard women say concerning some talk show, "Oh, I just can't miss that. Do you know who's going to be on today?" It's a temptation. We didn't have TV when I was a young pastor's wife—it was just becoming popular. But when we did get one, I had to learn to discipline myself. TV is a robber of prayer time. You would do well to limit yourself—especially if you're having trouble developing a prayer life.

I think if we understood the immense importance of prayer, we'd be more likely to commit ourselves and to sacrifice whatever we must to make it the focus of our lives. We just don't realize the power within our grasp. Prayer is the secret to having success in the ministry. It is the secret to having a successful Christian life. In fact, prayer is the only way you can truly live the life that Christ wants you to live. For that reason alone, you should long to become a woman of prayer.

Every important work of God begins with prayer. A.J. Gordon, whom Chuck loves to quote, says, "You can do more than pray after you've prayed. But you cannot do more than pray until you have prayed." [4] That's a beautiful principle to remember. And I've seen it to be true. I've often said that the untold story of Calvary Chapel's growth has been its saturation in prayer. From the very beginning, we had men's and women's prayer meetings. I was the youngest in our women's group, and oh, how I loved to listen to those older saints pray! I learned so much about prayer by listening to them talk to God. I remember one woman who used to address Him as "Father dear." I just loved to hear her say that.

Often, young pastors' wives have not learned how to pray as they should, nor have they experienced the answers to prayer like some of the precious elderly saints. That was the case for me. Those women knew through experience how to pull down the power of God, and I learned by listening to them. Week after week we met in our tiny little church and prayed, "God, give us men who would be soldiers of the cross. Lord, set these men on high—all ten of them." That's how small we were. But we prayed for those ten men. We cried out to God on their behalf—and He answered! I could hardly believe my eyes as I watched God mature and strengthen those men and fill them with His power. Through that group, God started a Saturday night men's prayer meeting. And God began to bless that little church and bring the people in—all because of prayer.

If it weren't for prayer, I never would have had the strength to endure all I have in the ministry. I mean that with all my heart. I remember what it was like, before we came to Calvary Chapel, to be in a church of 200 and watch it dwindle down to fifty. If you're the pastor's wife in a small church, take heart. I know how hard that can be. I would listen to Chuck and think what a wonderful teacher he was and how well he shared the Word, and watch week by week families leave our church. I was so confused and discouraged by that. I remember meeting for an all-day prayer meeting with five or six other women. We fasted all day and prayed for our church. Little did I know then that God was using this failure to mold and humble Chuck—to prepare him for all that was to come when we moved to Calvary Chapel and began to minister to the hippies. Chuck never would have walked in the humility he walks in today had he not walked through those early years. It was one of the most painful things I have ever experienced, but God brought me through it. In my times of prayer, God continued to uphold me despite the confusion and the pain.

I learned the secret of praying right at the beginning of our ministry. Things were often bleak, and I felt desperate so much of the time. Twice, Chuck decided to move us within three weeks of giving birth. It isn't easy to have a brand new baby and try to adjust to a new congregation at the same time. One of those moves was to a little concrete room that was behind the church, where our only running water came through a spigot in the wall. We didn't have a bathroom, so we had to use the restroom in the church. There wasn't a shower, so we had to go across the street to bathe at the neighbor's house. And we didn't have a sink, so I would have to heat pot after pot of water and pour it into a basin to give the baby a bath. We got pretty good at brushing our teeth out on the back porch with just a cup of water.

In our one-room concrete house, we figured out a way to hang curtains to divide the room into two living spaces. And our furniture—oh, that was a trial all of its own. Someone gave us a mohair couch ... have you ever sat on a mohair couch? It is just the yuckiest, most unpleasant material you can imagine. I had to put sheets over it to use it.

Even though we were young at the time, the ministry was physically taxing. We held seventeen services every week. In that first year, I was dragging my baby around everywhere we went—on hospital visits or at the park playing the organ twice a week in 110-degree heat. I'm truly not painting it blacker than it was. I reverence God far too much to ever say something that can't be substantiated.

But it wasn't just our physical conditions that drove me to prayer. We brought all our spiritual battles to the Lord too. We had to pray people into the church and sometimes we had to pray them out, because some people came in with their false doctrine. One man even told Chuck, "I'm going to see you in your coffin if you don't start preaching this doctrine." We were twenty-two years old. When you're that young and you have no idea what to do with such a threat, you pray. So we did. Chuck kept preaching the Bible, and the man who threatened him died shortly thereafter of a brain tumor.

Prayer not only protects us from warfare—and actually battles on our behalf—but it also is the primary means in advancing the kingdom of God. One time I felt an overwhelming burden to pray for the women of Calvary Chapel. For two days, I could do nothing else. I didn't care if I ate or slept. All I could do was pace the floor and pray. I kept asking, "God, what do You want for the women? What do You want us to do? How can we meet their needs?" As I prayed, God spoke very specifically to my heart. He told me I was to hold prayer meetings every Wednesday in April, in addition to our usual Monday morning prayer meetings. So that's what we did.

Near the end of April, God gave me another specific instruction. He told me I was to teach on the book of Esther during our Friday morning Bible study. And by the way, the reason I can remember these things so clearly is because I wrote each impression down in a journal— something I strongly urge you to do as well. I want to remember when the Lord speaks to me, and if He should tarry, I want my children and grandchildren to know in the years to come.

On Friday of that week, I spoke about Esther's desperation for her people, and her willingness to hazard her own life for their sake. "If I perish, I perish," she said. Then I felt impressed by the Lord to challenge our women: "I want each of you to covenant before the Lord to meet with at least one other woman each week to pray for one hour. You can pray over the phone, or you can meet in your car, or in a park, or at one of your homes. But wherever you meet, pray together for one hour,

because God tells us in His Word, 'If two of you agree on earth about anything you ask for, it will be done for you by My Father in heaven'" (Matthew 18:19).

A large group of women accepted that challenge. We covenanted together, and things began to happen. Husbands came to Christ. Alcoholics were delivered. Relationships were restored. Testimony after testimony came in about the wondrous things God was doing in our midst. One of the sweetest testimonies came on a Saturday morning when I was reading the local newspaper and I saw a picture of one of our pastors down at the beach baptizing hundreds of kids.

I said, "Chuck, I didn't know we were having a beach outreach."

He said, "I didn't either."

After church the next morning, a girl named Veronica came up to me. She said, "Kay, do you remember when you challenged us a few months ago to get together with one friend and pray for an hour each week? Well, I did that. The burden on my heart was for the kids at the beach. I would see them just standing around smoking pot … and the girls had no modesty whatsoever. I couldn't stand all their skimpy bathing suits." This was coming from a darling girl with a gorgeous figure, whom God had simply burdened with this issue.

"I kept seeing these young kids being pulled in by Satan, and so my prayer partner and I asked God for a big beach outreach. We just kept praying for that. Finally we shared with the pastor doing the Saturday night concerts and he said, 'Right on, I want to do it.' As it turned out, hundreds of kids showed up at that beach outreach, and many of them came to the Lord and were baptized." All this because Veronica and her friend had covenanted to pray for the kids on the beach.

Do you see what prayer can do? If we would just commit ourselves to prayer, we could shake the foundations of the earth. We can do it. And you can be a pastor's wife who inspires others to take up the cause of prayer.

You may not be aware of how sensitive your people are toward you. They can tell by your behavior, your reactions, your love, your compassion, your responses, your choices, and your conversations whether or not you're a woman of prayer. It's obvious to them. It's obvious to anybody with any spiritual sensitivity. I can talk with someone for just a short period of time and tell whether she goes into her prayer closet or not. There's a oneness of spirit that tells me. And your people can tell too.

I can't survive without prayer. I am a miserable, obnoxious wretch unless I spend time communing with the Lord. Now, I might be all right for a few days and be sunny and nice to the people in my life ... but beyond that, I cannot do it. Without prayer I am nothing of what God wants me to be. And neither are you.

The fact is, prayer fits us for our ministry to the church. It prepares us for the tasks God has called us to by causing our hearts to beat in synch with His. Do you know one of the reasons I know this to be true? Chuck prayed and sought God when we first came to Calvary Chapel, and God directed him to teach through the book of 1 John, the book of love. For the entire first year, this was the focus of our Sunday sermons. Love, love, love. We needed it. And so did the twenty-five squabbling people God had entrusted to us. You never saw a group of people so bent on fighting with one another. It's true. I think in part they had felt unloved before we came, so they acted in ignorance. They did not know how to love each other. But through prayer, Chuck had discovered God's heart for that group of people, and so Sunday after Sunday he spoke to them about love.

Now, here's the thing. If it had been me—if I had gone into that church knowing what I knew about their relationship with one another—I think I would have chosen another passage. I would have preached on something entirely different, like perhaps the passage about Euodia and Syntyche. I might have used that to give them a stern exhortation about getting along with one another. But Chuck prayed, and God chose the topic of love for our congregation.

Why did God lead him to that? Because in a very short time, God was going to bring in a tide of hippies through our door. Do you know the reaction a group of elderly, straight-laced people have toward hippies? Let me tell you. I'll never forget that first Sunday morning when those kids walked in and we could all hear the bells on the bottom of their jeans. The entire church stiffened. Up until that time, nobody came to church in jeans. You just didn't do it. That was considered a sin. But God had prepared the hearts of our people so that after a few minor adjustments, Chuck's teachings about love enabled everyone to see each other through God's eyes. The stiffening? That was just temporary. It was a reflex. But at their core, our people had learned to love. They reached out to the hippies who began to flock to our church, and they loved them to Jesus. This never would have happened if God had not led Chuck through prayer.

Prayer is vital and necessary—it is the power of God for the work of the ministry. But how do you set about praying? The more you pray, the more God will direct you to pray. I have some suggestions to help you get started. At the top of the list, pray for your husband and his ministry.

PRAY FOR GOD TO SHOW YOUR HUSBAND WHAT TO PREACH.

Only God knows what your church needs to learn. Pray for God to give your husband a sensitivity to the specific needs of your church.

PRAY THAT GOD WILL STRENGTHEN HIM IN TIMES OF TEMPTATION.

No matter how well you know your husband, you don't know him as well as God does. Only God sees his heart. Only God knows those things that will test and tempt him. Only God knows his greatest weaknesses. We can't know those things. But we can pray and ask God to strengthen him in all those areas.

PRAY FOR GOD TO REVEAL YOUR HUSBAND'S DEEPEST SPIRITUAL NEEDS.

Ask God to show you those things so you can pray for them specifically. I used to collect cartoons about pastors and pastors' wives. Some of them were very funny. I remember one that showed a picture of a pastor in a pot of water over a fire, surrounded by cannibals. They were cooking him up for lunch. And standing there with the cannibals was the pastor's wife. With her hands on her hips, she says to him, "Frankly, I didn't care much for that sermon either." I thought that was very funny—but it's not so funny when that's your attitude in real life. You don't need to know your husband's weaknesses so you can jump on them, but rather to lift them up to God.

PRAY THAT GOD WILL FILL YOUR HUSBAND WITH KNOWLEDGE, WISDOM AND UNDERSTANDING.

Quite some time ago, God gave me Colossians 1:9 for Chuck. I've been praying that verse for him ever since. It's a good verse for every pastor to minister effectively:

> For this reason we also, since the day we heard it, do not cease to pray for you, and to ask that you may be filled with the knowledge of His will in all wisdom and spiritual understanding.

Sometimes women can be very critical of their husbands in prayer. Instead of praying good things for him, she'll begin talking to God

about all the things she can't stand. "God, You see that crummy husband of mine. He likes secular music and he hasn't brought me flowers in ten years. Will You please make him a godly man for my sake?" But that's not how God wants us to pray. He wants us to set aside our critical attitudes and pray with concern. And I have found that praying this verse for Chuck kept me from ever being critical in my prayers.

Years after I began doing this, I received a little note in my box at church. It informed me about a lady who had just passed away and that God had given her Colossians 1:9 to pray for Chuck every day for years. I thought, *Oh, that's such a sweet confirmation, Lord.* But then I thought, *Why did You take her, Lord? I need her. I need her to be praying Colossians 1:9 with me.* I still continue to pray daily for Chuck to know God's will and to have the desire and the ability to do it. And I have consistently seen the fruit of that.

PRAY THAT HE IS AWARE OF GOD'S NEARNESS.

While praying for Chuck one time, I felt God impress upon me that He wanted Chuck to be aware that He was always with him. We know the Word tells us that God is always near, but sometimes we forget how ever-present He is. So I began praying that. Often, whenever God brings it to my mind, I'll stop whatever I'm doing and ask, "Lord, would You let Chuck just be very conscious of Your presence with him right now?"

PRAY THAT GOD KEEPS HIM FROM UNREASONABLE PEOPLE.

In 2 Thessalonians 3:1-2, Paul wrote,

> Finally, brethren, pray for us, that the word of the Lord may run swiftly and be glorified, just as it is with you, and that we may be delivered from unreasonable and wicked men; for not all have faith.

That warning is as true today as it was when Paul wrote it. We've had some of the strangest, most irrational, unreasonable people come around our church. Some have come to our church straight from a mental institution. We've had people show up in all sorts of costumes, claiming to be all sorts of men. "Elijah" has visited us many times. We've even had "Jesus the Messiah" visit over and over, but since we didn't recognize him, he pronounced us to be anti-Christ. These unstable and unreasonable people have called our church switchboard numerous times. They've even shown up at our house more times than I'd like to tell you. In fact, it's happened so often that I can no longer open the front door in the daytime if I'm alone in the house. We've had to remove our address from the phone book and get an unlisted number. We don't like it, but that's the way it is. That's part of the walk. And that's the easy part in a lot of ways. They can't harm us. We're God's children and He protects us—and I praise Him for that.

Still, I am very careful to pray that Chuck will be kept from unreasonable people. And even with the wide variety of odd people who have shown up over the years, one of our board members said for a church our size, we've had less problems than any church he knows. I'm certain it's the power of prayer that keeps us from being overrun with them.

PRAY THAT HE WILL GROW.

This may seem like a given, but we want to pray that our husbands never stop growing in their faith. Colossians 1:10 says it beautifully:

> And we pray this in order that you may live a life worthy of the Lord and may please Him in every way: bearing fruit in every good work, growing in the knowledge of God (*NIV*).

Pray that God will grow your husband up in all ways: in his faith, in the assurance of his calling, in his boldness, in his preaching, and in his love

for the people. Pray specifically about these areas, and add your own as the Lord reveals them to you.

PRAY THAT HE WILL SEEK GOD IN ALL HIS DECISIONS.

My husband has to make snap decisions every single day, and your husband does too. Pray that he isn't led by his emotions, his logic or his own preferences. Pray that he will remember to stop and seek God's will before he answers. Proverbs 3:6 promises us God will guide us when we include Him in our decisions. "In all your ways acknowledge Him, and He shall direct your paths."

PRAY THAT HE WILL GIVE WISE COUNSEL.

Every one of us has been guilty of giving bad counsel at one time or another. It's heartbreaking when someone takes advice from you and then you have to watch the effect it has on their lives. Pray that God will give your husband wisdom. Ask God to cause His words to flow through your husband to the people who come to him for advice.

PRAY THAT HE WON'T BE DECEIVED.

Oh, how Satan loves to deceive pastors. If he could, Satan would have our husbands preach from the pulpit something that isn't right, or say something that would offend the congregation and displease the Lord. Now, more than ever before, we need to pray that our husbands' eyes are firmly fixed on the truth of God's Word, and that they never succumb to the winds of false doctrine sweeping through the church. Pray that God protects your husband from the deceptive tactics of the enemy. Pray that he continues to be committed to teaching sound doctrine.

These are just some things you can and should be praying for your husband. It is so vital to serve him in this way. As his helpmate, this is your responsibility. He needs your prayer covering.

Your church needs your prayer covering as well. Pray for your entire congregation, but pray especially for the women of your church. Ask God to reveal to you their temptations, their struggles, and their deepest needs. Ask Him to show you how you can best minister to them and encourage them. Stand in the gap and cry out on their behalf, "Oh God, what are my women going through? What are these little lambs up against? Where are the wolves coming in? How is the world tugging at their hearts today? How much of the world are they absorbing through television, movies and books? What are they feeding their minds with? What influences are shaping their values and morals?"

Oh, love your women. Pray for them. Be willing to make a sacrifice of your time to care for them through prayer. It requires a sacrifice of your time. It seems that all the earth-shattering needs come in unexpectedly, don't they? And they so often come in at inconvenient moments. The phone rings, and it's a devastated woman calling to tell you her husband just left. She needs your prayers, and she needs them on the spot.

Sometimes we'll hang up from a phone call like that and we'll think, *I really need to spend more time praying with her than that. I need to go spend an hour in prayer for this situation ... but I'm right in the middle of cooking dinner.* Listen, prayer isn't something that only happens on our knees. Prayer can happen while we're cooking dinner or tending to little ones or vacuuming the house. Find time later to get on your knees for your friend, but in the meantime pray, "God, please undertake this situation." Maybe it's just a twenty-second prayer. That's all right. Just don't neglect to pray. Every time she comes into your mind, pray again.

Pray for your husband, pray for your congregation, and then, pray for yourself. You need it too. As pastors' wives, we need prayer desperately. The problems of the people can be overwhelming, and we can feel

inadequate to handle them. Sometimes people will walk up to us and share a horrible problem, and our minds will go blank. We want to reach out, but we can't think of the first thing to say. I've learned to simply take their hands and pray with them. It's the best thing I can do for them—much better than anything I could say.

Sometimes our struggle is personal. As close as we are with the Lord and as much good teaching as we get on a regular basis, it is still possible as a pastor's wife to be so overwhelmed with your own pain that you begin to think you can't go on. I think we would all be surprised if we learned how many pastors' wives have felt suicidal. It's probably not surprising when you consider how frantic Satan is to destroy our husbands and our families and our churches. He'd love to hurt all those people by hurting us. He would kill us himself if he could—but he can't. So he whispers to us, "Wouldn't it be nice to be done with all this? Wouldn't it be great to just fall asleep and never wake up?" When those thoughts come to you, remember that they are coming from the pit of hell.

Discouragement will come. At times, you will feel downhearted and defeated. But don't succumb to Satan's lies. Instead, bring all your dark thoughts to God. "Lord, I'm discouraged. I'm tired. I need more affection from my husband. I need to know the people love me." Whatever it is, bring it to Jesus.

You know, there have been times when I have prayed, "Please Lord, would You let somebody say something nice about me to Chuck today?" Sometimes I just need to know they care—and more than that, I want Chuck to be encouraged by hearing that the people care. And God has honored my prayer. Chuck will come home just beaming, and he'll tell me about a conversation he had with someone and the nice thing they said about me. "They sure do love you," he'll tell me. I'm so thankful when that happens. Your husband needs to hear good things about you. It doesn't matter if you've been married two years or ten years or a hundred years, like me … it's good for your husband to have a fresh appreciation for you. It makes you a little more special to him when he sees you through someone else's eyes. You can ask God to cause that to happen.

This is not an all-inclusive list—not by any means. If you're a mama or a grandma, pray for your little ones. Pray for your coworkers, if you've got them. Pray for your neighbors. We all have them. Pray for your community, and for our lost world. Pray for every single thing God places on your heart. You can't spend too much time in prayer. You simply can't. Do you know what I'm shocked about? In the short amount of time that I have prayed, God has done so much. It makes me wonder, *What if I spent four hours a day in prayer … or twelve? What might God do then?*

I want Him to stir my heart to pray more and more. And I want that for you too. No matter the condition or the size of your church, get on your knees as an intercessor. Pray down God's power on behalf of your people, and watch Him work.

I could write so much more about prayer. I don't even want to leave this subject, to be honest with you. But let me give you this one final thought: persevere. Whatever you do, don't give up on your prayers. And don't let yourself become rebellious toward prayer, even when it seems like nothing is changing.

A while back I'd been praying for a certain couple for years and years and years. Things would get a tiny bit better, and then they would get worse. It just continued on like that. One day, Chuck took a phone call from one of them. When he hung up and told me what was going on

between the two, I said, "I am so sick and tired of praying for them. I'm not going to pray this time."

Oh, how quickly rebellion can creep into our hearts. I didn't even realize it. I was angry and frustrated that two people who knew better weren't behaving as they should and weren't committed to one another as they should be. While in that state of frustration, I walked up to my room. But on the way, Luke 18:1 came to mind. "Men always ought to pray, and not lose heart."

I said, "Lord, I'm tired … and I feel like I'm losing heart."

Then I heard Galatians 6:9. "And let us not grow weary while doing good, for in due season we shall reap if we do not lose heart."

"Lord," I said, "You know I have prayed and prayed. I've written whole prayer journals on this couple." I still didn't want to pray. I was so disgusted, all I wanted to do was sleep. But I was so burdened that I couldn't sleep. So I sat up in bed—but I still wasn't going to pray.

Chuck had just recently returned from one of his trips, and he had brought home a little card that read, "Expect a miracle." Now, I don't like cards like that. I don't know why, but I don't. So I had thrown it on the bed after he gave it to me—when he wasn't looking. Here I am, sitting up in bed feeling frustrated and angry and more than a little stiff-necked, and I glanced down next to me and I see the words, "Expect a miracle." My first thought was, *Didn't I throw that in the trash*? I got out of bed and I picked it up to take it to the trash can, and the Spirit of God hit me. Ka-pow! "Kay Smith, you are rebellious. You are out of the will of God, and you are not pleasing His heart. Now, expect a miracle."

I took a big breath, and then I confessed my rebellious attitude to the Lord. I repented, and then I started praying. And just before I turned off the light, I set that card on my nightstand so when I woke up the next morning it would be the first thing I saw. In the morning, when the sun hit the room, I glanced over and saw those words. "Expect a miracle." I said, "Today there's going to be a miracle, God. I know there's going to be a miracle." My faith was lifted. And that day God worked a miracle. Those two people who had been so very far from one another walked into church together and sat down next to me. Earlier they had declared they would never be in a church again. God worked. It was a genuine miracle.

Maybe there's a little rebellion in your heart. Maybe you read these words and you say, "Well, after all, she's been in the ministry sixty-two years. She ought to pray. That's what old ladies do. And when I get old, I'll be a woman of prayer too."

Listen, you start right now. You start this day because you love the Lord, you love your husband and your children, and you love the people in your church. Stir up others to prayer by sharing all the answers God gives you. Tell your children every time God answers your prayers so that their faith is built up and they'll learn to bring their own needs to Him. This is so important. Every time our children were hurt, we laid hands on them and prayed for them. Not only does this build their faith, but I learned they will also stop crying a lot quicker when you do this.

Oh, the immeasurable power of prayer … how little we realize the gift we've been given. If we could only see with spiritual eyes what God does with our prayers, we would probably spend the rest of our days on our knees.

We once met a woman in Norway who had spent most of her adult life as a missionary to the Chinese. She was a large, big-boned woman, and very tall—and the Chinese took to calling her Big Annie. When we met her, she had come home to Norway to retire. She told us a story about something that happened to her years earlier when the Communists took over China and she was trying to cross the border. While the border guard searched her, he dug into her purse and pulled out a letter some friends had written to her in which they mentioned the Communists and called them the "Red Devil." Annie knew if the soldier read that letter, he would execute her on the spot. So she began to pray, "God, if there's anybody in Norway praying for me, let them pray now."

Well, as it happened, the soldier was illiterate. He couldn't read or write. So he took the letter and started up the stairs to his commanding officer. Annie watched him go and kept praying. Just as he neared the top of the stairs, the door opened and five soldiers bolted down the stairs. One of them looked and saw Annie, and said, "Big Annie, what are you doing here?" As a little boy, this soldier had been in Annie's orphanage.

She answered, "I'm trying to get across the border."

"What's stopping you?" he asked.

"That soldier found a letter in my purse but he couldn't read it so he's taking it up to the commanding officer."

The fellow replied, "What? Oh, give me that letter. That's just Big Annie. She's fine. Let her go across the border."

So Annie made it across the border and eventually back home to tell her story. After she finished sharing with her church in Norway what had happened, some people came up to her and asked, "Do you have any idea what time that happened?"

She said, "Yes, I wrote it down in my journal." She told them the exact date and time God had intervened.

The family went home to check their own prayer journal and discovered that at the exact moment this was happening to Annie, which was at 3:00 a.m. in Norway, their five-year-old boy had awakened. He went into his parents' room, shook them awake and said, "Pray for Big Annie. She's in trouble."

His parents said, "We'll pray. You go back to bed now."

But he wouldn't let it go. "You've got to pray for Big Annie—she's in trouble!"

So finally, his parents said, "All right." They took his hands and started to pray. But he insisted, "She's really in trouble. Jesus woke me up and told me to pray. Big Annie's in trouble. Please get down on your knees and pray for Big Annie." So his parents got out of bed, and together the family got on their knees and prayed for Big Annie. And God spared her life.

Beloved, I beseech you again: commit yourself to prayer. Be the kind of mother who raises up children who understand the power of prayer, and be the kind of wife who covers her husband in prayer. Just by your example alone, be the kind of pastor's wife who influences her entire congregation to get on their knees. There's no greater gift you can give to the people God has entrusted to you.

Chapter Three

SUBMITTED IN MARRIAGE

THREE WEEKS after we moved to Prescott, Arizona, Chuck turned to me one morning and said, "I'm going to move that rock away from the church so we can build an addition on the side."

"You're what?" I asked. I heard him the first time but I just couldn't believe what I'd heard. The rock was gigantic—more of a boulder actually. It was much bigger than Chuck. In fact, it was almost half the size of the church building. And it perched on a hill just above the left-hand side of this little framed church.

Now, Chuck is a doer. It's really incredible how much energy he has, even to this day. He just goes and goes and makes everyone around him tired. Once he gets an idea in his head, and he's sure it's a good idea, there's no talking him out of it. Still I tried.

The Privilege

We stood together on the hill studying the boulder—Chuck with a crowbar and me with a madly beating heart. Chuck was eyeing the best spot to stick his crowbar, but I was looking at the direction I was sure that boulder would take once he loosened it.

"Chuck, you can't do this," I cautioned.

He'd already stuck the crowbar under it and had begun pushing.

"Chuck … it's going to roll right into the side of the church!"

"No," he answered. "I've got this."

But I had a different angle of the situation—a much *better* view, in my opinion. I could see exactly what was going to happen. And I thought, *We are equal in this relationship. I can have my say-so … and I say it's going through the church.* So I warned him one more time.

Once more Chuck disagreed. "It's not going through the church. Just stand back."

Chuck pushed again and the rock started to roll. My heart was in my throat, but then … the rock just stopped. And I thought, *Oh, God is with us! The rock stopped! He's going to bless this ministry forever …* And with that, the rock rolled off the mound, down the hill and right through the side of the church. That whole wall exploded inwardly, and the rock barreled over three rows of pews, barely missing a little heater on the left side of the room.

Chuck had been the pastor of that church for only three weeks. Stunned, we stared down at the carnage. Then I looked at Chuck and thought, *I married a maniac.*

He wasn't afraid at all. Surprised, maybe, but not afraid.

"How are you going to get that out?" I asked.

"I don't know … but I will."

The parsonage was down the street a little bit. Not sure what else to do, we walked back home. About two hours later, we got a call from the former pastor who also lived just a few blocks from the church. "Chuck," he said, "you will never believe what has happened. That giant rock rolled into the church!"

I learned many lessons about being a pastor's wife those first few weeks in Prescott, lessons that have stayed with me throughout my married life. One thing I realized is that I will never be able to control Chuck. I also learned that I married a man who has no fear. He trusts God, even when things look bleak. He trusts that God has a plan and that He will work it out in His own way. It turned out perfectly fine that the rock rolled through the church. We got our Sunday school addition, and probably much faster than we would have otherwise.

Still, it was an interesting way to learn submission. And it was just the beginning of a very interesting journey—a pilgrimage, if you will, because we are indeed on a pilgrimage. We are walking with our husbands through a land that is not our home, with one destination in mind: heaven.

The world, of course, doesn't view marriage as a pilgrimage. That's because most people in the world don't think about heaven at all. Therefore, their advice about marriage is all about the here and now. There's so much advice out there in books, magazines, on TV, and on the radio. You couldn't possibly live long enough to try it all. Besides, most of it doesn't work anyway.

Occasionally you do hear a bit of good advice. I once heard a conversation between a distraught wife and a "marriage expert" on the radio. The woman had a pretty big problem in her marriage—something she wasn't at all happy about—but when she finished explaining it to the "doctor," the advice she got was, "Well, you'll just have to get over it." She said it three times, in fact, because the dismayed caller kept arguing with her. "There's nothing else for you to do. You'll just need to get over it." I thought, *You know, that's pretty good advice.* There are so many things in life, and in a marriage, that you simply can't change. You might as well just get over it and move along.

God's Word is the only place where we can always find good, true, reliable advice on marriage. Two of my favorite verses on this subject are found in the book of Proverbs. These have been my guiding verses for marriage. "The wise woman builds her house, but the foolish pulls it down with her own hands" (Proverbs 14:1), and "Through wisdom a house is built, and by understanding it is established; by knowledge the rooms are filled with all precious and pleasant riches" (Proverbs 24:3-4). Isn't that glorious? If we want to build a solid marriage, we need wisdom, understanding, and knowledge. All those are found in the person of Jesus Christ.

First Peter 3:1 is also precious to me, although it took a while to realize it actually applied to me.

> Wives, likewise, be submissive to your own husbands, that even if some do not obey the word, they, without a word, may be won by the conduct of their wives.

As a young pastor's wife, whenever I began to read 1 Peter 3, I would zip right through those first verses. My husband is a Christian, so I assumed they didn't pertain to me.

When I was twenty-five years old, I sat under the teaching of an "older" woman, who was probably forty or forty-five. I remember when she got to this passage she said, "You know, Christians just skip over this part thinking it isn't speaking to them. But think about this: most of the things your husband might do which would cause trouble are 'disobedient to the Word.' If they don't obey the Word, what are you going to do?"

I went home and I thought about what it would mean to me as a wife if my husband were to stop being obedient to the Word. As I studied it over and over, I asked God to help me work out my part in my life. All these years later I'm still studying this passage and asking God for that help. I never want to stop growing into the wife Chuck needs me to be. And since only God knows what Chuck really needs, I must stay close to the Lord to seek His guidance daily.

Peter inserts the word "likewise" in that first verse in chapter 3 because he just spent half of chapter 2 teaching about submission to authority. Now he turns his attention to wives, and he tells us, "Wives, likewise, be submissive to your own husbands." We all submit to authority every single day, don't we? We stop at red lights instead of just speeding through. We pay our taxes. We obey all kinds of rules that we don't grumble and gripe about—or at least, we shouldn't. But when we read 1 Peter 3, somehow the words "submissive" and "obey" stand out to us in horrible, bold, capital letters. In our minds, the instruction turns into an impossible, distasteful thing, and we think, *That's absolutely the last thing I want to do.*

Our flesh is to blame for that. Although we don't rebel against stoplights and taxes (at least not much), there's something within our human nature that rebels against submission to our husbands.

Our culture doesn't help any. We live in a time when women demand empowerment. They don't want to be a helpmate to a man. But when God took the rib out of Adam to create Eve, He didn't say, "Now, get out there and fight some wars with him." Instead He said, "You are to be his helpmate." This in no way means that women are inferior. We're just as important as men are in God's plan. But He had an order for a perfect plan—an order of authority. I believe He meant for the women to be in the home and raise the babies, and for the man to be out there providing for his family. He made us smaller, as a rule, and not quite as strong as men. But there's a tremendous battle against God's plan today. And whenever we embrace the truth of 1 Peter 3, we run counter to the culture.

First Peter 3:7 contains another "likewise":

> Husbands, likewise, dwell with them with understanding, giving honor to the wife, as to the weaker vessel, and as being heirs together of the grace of life.

How beautiful that is! Stop for a moment and bow your heart before the Lord. Thank Him for making you and your husband heirs together of the grace of life.

Backing up a little to verse 3, Peter describes the behavior of this woman in verse 1:

> Do not let your adornment be merely outward—arranging the hair, wearing gold, or putting on fine apparel—rather let it be the hidden person of the heart, with the incorruptible beauty of a gentle and quiet spirit, which is very precious in the sight of God (1 Peter 3:3-4).

It's interesting to me that after Peter gives us this exhortation, he refers back to Sarah.

For in this manner, in former times, the holy women who trusted in God also adorned themselves, being submissive to their own husbands, as Sarah obeyed Abraham, calling him lord, whose daughters you are if you do good and are not afraid with any terror (1 Peter 3:5-6).

As I've read these verses over and over and over again, I believe that every verse in 1 Peter 3:1-6 exemplifies Sarah. This is the way she conducted herself, and we are her daughters if we do likewise. As women of God and as pastors' wives, we're to follow these godly principles.

If you want to follow these principles, you'll need to stand strong. Be prepared for ridicule, because the world loves to make fun of Christians who actually live according to God's standards. But what does it matter how the world views you if, by obeying, you please the heart of God?

Now, as I look at all the different married couples in Scripture, it's interesting to me that God chose Abraham and Sarah to be our example. They had some real issues in their marriage at times. I've wondered why the Lord didn't choose Zacharias and Elizabeth. They were blameless. They loved God and always walked in His ways. Why didn't He choose Elkanah and Hannah? Peninnah was a bit of a problem, but Elkanah loved Hannah deeply. When he said, "Am I not better to you than ten sons?" (1 Samuel 1:8) that's pretty good talk. I like that about Elkanah. And Hannah was obviously a woman of prayer. Wouldn't they have made good role models? Or how about Aquila and Priscilla? Now, there was a great marriage. They worked side by side ministering to people and making tents. And when she ministered to Apollos, he didn't have a bit of problem with that.

So with these other couples in the Scriptures, why do you suppose God chose Abraham and Sarah to be our role models? I believe God chose

this couple precisely because they were so flawed. Think about the mistakes the two of them had made. Abraham tried to pass Sarah off as his sister—not once, but twice. Later, becoming impatient with God's timing, Sarah encouraged Abraham to take her handmaid, Hagar, for a concubine so they could finally have a child. Ishmael was the result. And when God revealed to Abraham in Genesis 17 that He would bless him with a son through Sarah—who was ninety then—Abraham laughed in disbelief and offered a more logical solution. "Oh God, let Ishmael live before You." This from the great man of faith! Sarah herself laughed when the Lord told her she would have a baby. Since no one had heard except God, when He asked Abraham, "Why did Sarah laugh?" she tried to deny it. She lied to God.

They didn't behave perfectly. We don't either, which is why we can relate to them so well. We make a lot of mistakes and our husbands make a lot of mistakes. Nevertheless, along with the mistakes, Sarah did many things right in her marriage. These are what we want to bring into our own marriages. What we learn about Sarah is her subjection and obedience to her husband.

Now, as I mentioned, we have a tendency to hate those words before we even have a chance to operate in them. In a wedding ceremony the bride's veil flutters a little bit when the pastor says, "Love, honor, and obey." We just don't like the sound of those words. But I think the husband's task from Ephesians 5 is much harder. He is told to love his wife and give himself for her as Christ did the church.

None of us are always in subjection as we should be, and our husbands don't always give themselves for us as Christ did the church. But it's a call from the Lord. The question we need to ask ourselves is: Do I love Jesus enough to be obedient? Can I obey His words here in 1 Peter?

Instead of letting my flesh rise up and argue, can I love Jesus enough to obey my husband when he makes a decision I don't like?

You know, whenever I'm preparing to teach, I end up being tested in that subject first—it never fails. Don't you find that to be true? That's exactly what happened when I was preparing to speak at our pastors' wives' conference on the subject of submission.

Because of a big remodeling project, we had been out of our home for a little over a year at that point. Just as we finished the remodel, Chuck decided he wanted to add a room on top of the garage so we could have a bigger office. We'd been using just two tiny bedrooms for offices. It was a great idea, except the City rejected the plans. I have to admit that I was secretly thrilled, because it meant we could move back home. I had been missing my house and longed to be home. I have a piano there, and when things get tough, I play and sing to Jesus. But just as I was gearing up to move back home, Chuck found another way to add on this room.

My heart fell. I knew they were going to have to break through a wall into my office in order to add on the room. Even though we were not living in the house, I could still go over there and get books out of my library when I needed them. I'd pick up a book or two when I went to get the mail, and then bring them back again on another trip.

Now, this was two weeks before our pastors' wives' conference. Not only that, but I had two other retreats *and* our Joyful Life Bible study was just about to start back up. I needed my books. So I didn't ask Chuck—I begged him. "Oh, Honey, please! Please don't do that until all three retreats are over. I'm over my head right now! I'll move it all—just let me take care of it after the retreats!"

And because I know that Chuck understands things better visually, I threw in a picture for him as well. "Chuck," I said, "these days I am like a barren tree. There is nothing on it but one little withered leaf with a very short stem, and I'm just barely hanging on in a windstorm." I really gave it my best shot. Chuck didn't say much. He sort of acknowledged that he heard me, but he didn't say much. I should have known.

A few days later, while we were having dinner, Chuck said, "You know what? You only have to move those clothes out of the closet in your office. I already packed everything else into boxes and moved them."

I said, "What?"

He told me again. I literally went into shock. All I could think about was how my desk had been set up just so, and I knew where everything was. I had special little treasures, special boxes....

In my whole life, I have never had a reaction like that. Here we were, sitting together at dinner, and I couldn't move. I sat there frozen. I couldn't react. I couldn't speak—or cry. I didn't say anything, but I sure did think, *He couldn't have. He wouldn't. He didn't.*

Well, wouldn't you know it—the phone rang. Doesn't it always happen precisely during the most traumatic moments of life? The person calling was someone who always talks a long time to Chuck.

Somehow I managed to get up and walk over to a little couch we had. As I sat there, I first thought how much I wished I could tell the person on the phone, "Hang up now," although I wasn't thinking it in nice terms like that. I was very much in the flesh.

I probably sat there for ten minutes before I finally started talking to God about it. "Lord, You've got to help me." That's all I could say, because I was so overcome by the thought of all the books I was going to need in the coming weeks, and how I wasn't going to be able to find them now.

After I had sat quietly for another ten minutes or so, God spoke to my heart and I heard Him say, "Kay, is this eternally important?"

Of course, it wasn't.

Then He asked, "Do you want to do My will or yours?"

My heart began to melt.

And then He asked me a third question. "Is this more important than your relationship with Chuck?"

I knew it wasn't. And as I sat on the couch, the peace of God came over me so powerfully. It was the peace that Philippians 4:7 promises—the peace that transcends all human understanding.

When Chuck's telephone conversation ended, we went back to the dining table together and talked while we ate. I still wanted to discuss the books, but I wanted to wait for the right moment. Instead we talked about his phone call and a few other things.

It wasn't until after the dishes were done and I was getting ready to fold some laundry that I finally brought up the subject. Chuck was reading at the table and I set the clothes down. As I was folding one of his T-shirts, I looked at him and said those words no husband ever likes to hear, "Honey, could we talk about this?" Does your husband like that? No. As a rule, they hate it though we say it really sweetly.

Do you know what he did? He reached out and he put his hand on top of mine and said, "Honey, I understand. I really understand." And he did. I knew he did.

You know, I could have sat on a nest of thorns and carried on a bit. "Poor me." Or I could have moped around unhappily and punished him with my silence for days. You know the way we act sometimes. But I didn't. All I said was, "Well, whatever you do, please don't touch the linen closet!" The construction men were going to have to go through the bedroom wall to build the addition, and I couldn't bear the thought of someone else packing up the linen closet. It held much more than just linens—it had everything in there. I knew exactly where every item was. So that was my only request—"Please, please don't touch the linen closet!" God's peace was there for me.

His peace was still with me when a few days later I learned from our cleaning lady that Chuck had emptied the linen closet.

"What?"

She nodded. "There's nothing in it."

For a split second I started in again. *He couldn't have. He wouldn't. He didn't.*

She asked—just teasing me, of course—"Have you ever felt like you wanted to divorce him?"

I said, "I can't believe he did this. I cannot believe he did this ..." Then, once again, God overwhelmed me with His peace. I told her, "I have the peace of God. This is so amazing. This is not Kay. This is not Kay. It can only be explained by the Lord!"

She replied, "You're some woman!"

I agreed—jokingly. But I knew that if my flesh had been actively alive and at work, I probably would have marched down to the church, where Chuck had stored all my things, and started dragging boxes back home.

This lesson in submission isn't one we learn overnight. It's a lesson we have to learn again and again. God will allow things to come up to show you where you're still trying to rule.

We were in the midst of a big redecorating project at the church. Once again, it was right in the middle of dinner when Chuck said, "We're going to pull up the carpet in the sanctuary."

We women have our territory, right? And wouldn't you say that redecorating is part of that territory? Well, I started thinking about carpet colors. "Oh good," I said. "It's about time. Did you bring home the carpet samples?"

"No," Chuck said. "I already ordered the carpet."

"You ordered …" I didn't even finish the sentence. I wanted to say, "You ordered it without me!" But I didn't.

After a minute I asked, "What color did you get?"

"I got the same."

Mauve? I thought, *Oh, not mauve again!*

Do you think 1 Peter 3:1 applies to that situation? It does. Chuck has the authority to order mauve carpet without my permission or my input.

The Privilege

I'm someone who likes to wait and think and mull over the choices—but I'm married to a man who wants the job done yesterday. The men ripped up the old carpet and had the new carpet installed within the week. And the new carpet was clean and it looked fine. Who cares about the color? Is that an eternal issue? No! Does God want me to be submissive and obedient to His will and in subjection to my husband? Yes. Is my relationship with Chuck more important than the carpet in the church? Yes. Yes. Yes. Yes.

If we want to be the daughters of Sarah, then we need to adorn ourselves with a gentle and quiet spirit, not with contentiousness. These are beautiful things to the Lord and an influence to our husbands. But too often, we settle for outward adornment.

I'm really not fond of going into cosmetics departments these days. They're so big and loaded with products. I sometimes end up going with my granddaughters, and every time I do, someone in the department wants to do a makeover on me.

Just buying lipstick is an ordeal. My granddaughters like to go through color after color after color. I grab one and go and hope it matches something I have at home.

We spend so much time on our lips, our hair and our clothes. We spend time exercising and getting manicures and pedicures. But sometimes we spend more time on our outward appearance than we do on our inward appearance—getting our heart right with God—walking with Him and adorning the inner person. We're built up every time we pick up His Word, or listen to good, solid Bible teaching, or sing a worship song. Not only do those things build us up, they also draw our husbands' hearts toward us.

Girls today put a lot of stock in sexy clothing. They think that's the way to get their husband to stick with them forever. But you know what? That doesn't last. It's great for a while, but it simply doesn't last. It takes far more than outer appearance to make a strong, united marriage.

In Titus 2:4, the older women are told to admonish the younger women to love their husbands. The word used for "love" in that verse is not *eros*, which means "passionate love"—a love based on physical or sexual attraction. The word God actually uses in this verse is *phileo*, which means "friendship love." We are to be a friend to our husbands. Can your husband say that about you? Would he call you his friend? Do you protect him around other people, or do you share all his failures with them? When you're with other women, do you criticize your husband?

If you are to have a heart like Sarah's, then you need to attend to the hidden person of the Lord and make it your goal to become your husband's closest friend. You need to support him in the decisions he makes and not contend over those things.

I've often wondered what was going through Sarah's mind the morning Abraham took Isaac up to Mount Moriah to slay him. We don't know for sure if she knew what Abraham was intending to do, but if she did, how do you think she would have reacted? How would you have reacted?

I have read that when God changed Sarah's name from Sarai to Sarah, it was done to indicate a change in her character. I have also read that Sarai means "contentious" while Sarah means "princess." You know what made the difference? God took the *i* out of her name and put the last two letters of *Jehovah* into her name. I like that. When the "I" is out of our lives—when we're dead to self—then we change from being contentious women to being the King's princesses.

If you read that and you immediately thought, *I still have "I" in my name,* then the answer is to go to Romans 6:11 and reckon yourself dead. You are dead to your flesh and alive unto Jesus. Then after the reckoning comes the walking. Determine to walk in the Spirit, obeying His will from this moment on.

There's something else about Sarah I'd like to point out. The Word tells us that not only was she in subjection to Abraham, but she also called him "lord." Now, that's "lord" with a small "l," not a capital "L." Do you know what that signified? It was a sign of respect. Men need our respect. Women need love, and that's why God told husbands to love their wives. But He told us to respect our husbands, because that's their greatest need.

How are you doing in this area? Do you respect your husband? Thankfully, in this day and age we don't have to go around calling our husbands "lord." That would be a little awkward. But we can show them respect in so many other ways. When we do, it pleases the Lord and it blesses those around us. It's never pleasant to be around cross, bossy, nagging wives. I think it's awful because it belittles their husbands.

As the handmaiden of the Lord, it's so important to set a good example, not just for the people in our church—who are definitely watching—but also for our children. They will imitate you. If you respect their dad, they will too. If you don't, they'll pick up on that as well. You are to influence your children to "honor their father and mother, that their days may be long upon the land" (Exodus 20:12). You may not always agree with your husband—but you must always show respect for him.

Now, Sarah did not have an easy life. Not in the least. She was a sojourner and a pilgrim, and she followed a husband who did not always make the best decisions. Hebrews 11:11 tells us how Sarah had the strength to faithfully submit. "By faith Sarah herself also received strength." She did it through faith. And faith, you know, is an action word. It's not just an inside-believing word. It spurs us to action.

A few verses later, Sarah is listed among those who died in faith. "These all died in faith, not having received the promises." Similarly, we haven't received eternal life yet either. We've received the promise, but we haven't moved into it yet. We're still pilgrims on the road. "But having seen them afar off were assured of them, embraced them and confessed that they were strangers and pilgrims on the earth" (Hebrews 11:13).

I'd like to ask you this: Are you assured that you're on your way to eternity and that God awaits you in heaven? Is that destination so continually before you that you're persuaded of its promise? Does the desire to see Jesus face to face press you forward on the path to heaven? And does the truth of eternity—and of arriving there with sheaves in your arms, the fruit of the life you've lived here on earth—motivate you to serve Him all the more fervently while you wait for that day?

We've been given a tremendous privilege as pastors' wives. The impact that we have on people will be largely affected by the answers we give to these questions. If we are not motivated by love for Jesus and a desire to bless and serve Him, our people will suffer.

I remember several years back when I heard about a pastor and his wife who left one church and moved to another. After they were gone, several people from that first fellowship gave a report about what happened there. They painted a picture of how the pastor's wife had acted and it seemed that she had not been a blessing or a godly influence to them. It broke my heart. I didn't know the woman or the situation firsthand, and who knows, maybe the people were wrong. But what if they were

right? It grieved me to think that this woman might have squandered the privilege she had been given.

I think all of us who have been entrusted with that privilege should ask ourselves this question: If I moved on to another church, how do I want to be remembered? Meditate on that, and let it be a governing influence in your life. Will you leave the fragrance of Christ behind—or the scent of the flesh?

Right around the same time I heard about that pastor's wife, I received this letter from another. This was written by Gail Gonzales.

"It has been a long journey from that Sunday at Costa Mesa in 1980 when I gave my heart to the Lord. My marriage had been in a shambles, but Jesus turned our lives around in just a short time. Dave had gotten saved three months earlier. We were on our way to the most exciting, rewarding, and hardest years ahead. I always knew my worst Christian nightmare was to be a pastor's wife. You know, those women—nylons, high heels, dresses every Sunday. Oh, and they were always godly, with just the right answers. Weren't they? I could never fit. I was loud, dressed one step above a bag lady and always said what I thought. My foot was continually in my mouth. I told Dave, 'Thank goodness you're not a pastor.' Well, God had other plans for me. Dave became a senior pastor. We sold our home in Lakewood, put the dog and the baby in the U-Haul, and waved goodbye to our dear friends and family. We cried together as we pulled the truck out of the driveway and thought, *What are we doing?*

"Dave felt called to Wisconsin to start a church. He had no job, no elders, no one waiting there to help us—and no health insurance and no safety net. What I learned in the next six years was that God was to be our safety net. I learned that being a pastor's wife was not nylons and dresses. It was learning to be quiet and letting my husband lead. I also learned how cruel some people could be and how I had to lean on Jesus. Jesus taught me to forgive and not want to kill someone who had just said something horrible about my husband. The loneliness caused Dave and me to grow closer together—to become one another's best friend—but not without some really good fights first. I realized the enemy was for real and always ready to start something, either in our marriage or in our church. We made many mistakes in this church planting. There were blessings too—but mostly very hard work for Dave. Wisconsin was like a first child. You worry about everything and let every small thing concern you. Calvary Chapel Cerritos is like the second child. With it, you are relaxed and able to enjoy and have fun. It is such a blessing. Am I sorry I am a pastor's wife? Never. Would I have gone to Wisconsin if I'd known what was ahead of us? Probably not. However, I wouldn't trade those lessons learned now for a million dollars."

Quite unexpectedly, without any warning, a few short weeks after sending this letter, this pilgrim entered heaven. Gail is forever with Jesus now—but she left a beautiful legacy behind.

Make sure you leave a beautiful legacy too.

Chapter Four

THE HANDMAIDEN OF THE LORD

*Y*EARS AGO, while driving up to one of our women's retreats at Twin Peaks, my friend, Mary, and I came to a detour. I was in an awful hurry to get to the conference center and we had been making terrific time up to that point. I said, "Wait … what's this? Where is this detour taking us?" I knew that area well and I imagined driving miles and miles in the wrong direction. But as we drove along, we began to see the most colorful trees along the road, full of gorgeous fall leaves. It was just so beautiful! I found myself thinking, *Thank You, Lord, for this detour.* I said to Mary, "Oh, isn't the Lord good to slow us down and give us a detour?"

By the time we reached Twin Peaks my spirit had quieted down. I had enjoyed the beauty of God's creation and the blessing of His presence. I

was reminded of His power as He impressed upon me that the women I was going to minister to were His women and His workmanship, and that He would accomplish His work in and among us.

You and I might be known as "the wife of the pastor," but in reality, we truly are "handmaidens of the Lord." This means we don't question what God allows into our lives, whether that be detours, disappointments or difficult people. We understand we've been bought with a price, and our lives are no longer our own.

I think phone calls are one of the hardest detours in ministry. The phone never stops ringing and it doesn't care what else you had planned for the day. There have been many days when I couldn't get dressed until 3:00 in the afternoon unless I took the phone off the hook or just let it ring. The calls came in one right after the other. You can't afford to ignore a call because it could be an emergency. I remember many times standing in the kitchen making this certain cake we all loved. It always turned out light and fluffy and wonderful because you stood there and beat it for three whole minutes. I'd be beating it for about a minute, and the phone would ring. I'd think, *I'll just answer the phone real fast and get back to the cake.* The caller wouldn't start out with, "Hi! Are you busy right now? Is this a convenient time to talk?" Instead, she would blurt out, "Kay, I just found out my little girl is pregnant."

What do you do then? You forget the cake. God has just brought you a detour that is more important than your fluffy cake. The cake would be delicious, yes, but it would be devoured in one night and forgotten— except on the waistline. But touching that precious woman for Jesus and giving her the comfort, hope and help she needs will last for eternity. I really believe in eternity, maybe thousands of years after the event, God will remind us of something we did and how much it meant to Him.

"How you blessed My heart when you were willing to lay aside your plans." When we make our plans, we must always be ready to lay them aside when the Lord brings something else along.

Often when Chuck is away traveling, I have a whole list of fun things I like to do which he doesn't necessarily enjoy doing. I would plan to spend a whole evening reading a book or I might plan to go to a new restaurant or visit some place that would never interest Chuck. Now that my children are raised I can do those things sometimes. So I make my plans … and the phone will ring and the caller will say, "I know that Chuck is away and I thought this would be a good time for us to talk." I'll look over at the book waiting for me and then look at the clock and watch the hour fly by. And it can be hard. But after you've listened and ministered to that person, something in your heart tells you that the Lord had brought something far better than whatever you had planned. God is blessed by your willingness to walk in love toward others as you set your own plans aside.

When detours come along in life—and they will—thank God for them. He has most likely allowed them in order to do some special work. Or maybe it's to slow you down long enough that you would remember to praise His name.

Not only are there a lot of detours in the life of the pastor and his wife, there are also disappointments. Some of us went into the ministry starry-eyed, thinking, *Oh, God is with us and it's going to be wonderful, and He's going to go before us and smooth out every rough place.* Well, part of that is true. He is definitely with us, and He does go before us, but He doesn't necessarily smooth out every rough place. That's because the disappointment is going to do more for us than the smoothing out would. Those rough patches teach us to be steadfast.

Like David, we need to get to the place where we say, "My heart is fixed, O God, my heart is fixed: I will sing and give praise" (Psalm 57:7 *KJV*). When we say this, we declare before the Lord and His holy angels—as well as the enemy and his demons—that our hearts are steadfast. We are declaring that nothing will sway us from serving God. And the man or woman who makes a commitment to steadfastness will never be overthrown by evil circumstances. Psalm 112:7 promises that the one whose heart is fixed on the Lord, trusting in Him, will not be in fear of bad news or live in dread.

I've known of pastors' wives who come to a retreat so weary and overwhelmed that they wish they never, ever have to leave the retreat and return to their churches because there may be tension or difficult people back home. Well, according to that verse in Psalm 112, we don't have to fear bad news nor do we have to live in dread of what may happen. Instead, we must fix our hearts on the Lord.

Verse 8 goes on to say, "His heart is secure, he will have no fear; in the end he will look in triumph on his foes." How wonderful to be able to face your foes calmly! Most of us have to exercise the utmost control when dealing with foes. When your trust is in the Lord and your heart is steadfastly fixed, you don't have to be anxious or fearful when people come against you.

Every church has its share of rascals—unruly people who cause trouble without necessarily realizing it. But others are more purposeful about stirring up trouble. When they don't get their own way, they will set themselves against you or your husband and they might start a phone-calling campaign to spread hateful dissension to the rest of the body. Then there are others who will try to bring in false doctrine. That's the hardest thing for me. I have a very difficult time with the ones who try to lead the people astray.

Years ago, Gayle Erwin spoke at one of our pastors' conferences. He said something that has stuck with me—something that comes to mind whenever I have to deal with someone difficult. He said, "See every person as someone Christ died for." That has helped me tremendously. It also helps me to think toward heaven and realize that the one who seems so difficult now will be perfect there. We'll both be in our perfected states! That person is going to be so precious and wonderful then, and I'll probably want to spend all sorts of time talking and supping with him or her. It's just this old body of flesh we find ourselves in now—this tent—that makes it so hard to see the real person inside.

Have you ever gone camping in a rainstorm? What happens when all that rain accumulates outside the tent, and then someone inside touches the side of the tent? The rain comes pouring through. Then everybody is upset with the one who did it. In the life of a pastor's wife, there's always somebody like that on the inside of the tent who hits the side during a rainstorm. But you know what? God allows that person to be there for your growth and education. I believe I've learned more through the difficult ones than I have through the sweet, marvelous people. Those sweet ones have been an encouragement to me and have taught me wonderful things about the Lord, but the difficult ones always sent me to my knees. I think that's even more helpful.

God places impossible people in the tent with us and our natural inclination is to avoid them. Those are the ones you hope won't call. Before caller ID, all I could do was say, "You answer it, Honey. It might be her." That worked just fine when Chuck was home, but invariably one of those calls would come when he wasn't home, and I'd have to face it head on. That's when you start praying and looking for answers in God's Word. You have to. You can become a bitter, rebellious wretch if you don't seek God for answers as to how to handle those difficult people, and you will lose any influence you may have had in the church.

Now, this is not to say that you have to be a doormat. We are not called to be weak women. We are to be strong in the Lord and steadfast. There will be times to confront a situation or rebuke someone's behavior. But how are we to rebuke? We're to do it in love. I am so fearful of that word "rebuke." Every time I sense that the Lord is calling me to do it, I wait, wait, wait upon Him until He gives me the love to do it effectively. It's never had any lasting effect unless I did it in love. When I've corrected another person out of my own frustration or anger, it's done nothing but cause more trouble.

I think your own attitude toward the rebuke is very telling. If you can't wait to approach that person and let loose about how you feel, it's likely that you're doing it in a wrong spirit. But if you are reluctant or you flat out don't want to rebuke them, you've probably got the right attitude. I know those times when I've rebuked in love, I have gone to that person with great reluctance. Tears would be streaming down my face and I've often done more crying than talking. I'd just say, "I'm so broken over this and it's hard to say anything." And you know, they usually reach out and comfort me. "Oh Kay, I'm so sorry I did this and caused you grief." I wouldn't be crying on purpose or trying to manipulate the situation—it was simply the Lord working in my heart.

Please be careful about those times when you confront someone. Bathe the conversation in prayer before you go. Wait on the Lord for the right words, especially for the right attitude. Ask Jesus to fill your heart with love for that difficult person. Never confront someone unless the Holy Spirit puts it firmly upon your heart, and then it must be done in love.

Take a moment right now to think about the ones in your fellowship who always seem to be pushing against the side of the tent during a rainstorm. You know who they are. Consider each one and determine to see them as a challenge and not as a problem. Recognize you are the handmaiden of the Lord and that your loving Father has brought them to you for your own good so you will grow and mature. Ask God to show you how to deal with them in love. If it's necessary—and only if absolutely necessary—learn how to pray them *out* of the church.

Does that comment surprise you? Maybe you've never had a situation where that was required. But let me tell you, it happens. When it does, you will know the difference. The people we have asked God to remove from us were not those who were just a little bit difficult or unruly. These people were bent on destruction.

We once had a woman in our church who was absolutely determined to have Chuck for herself. She didn't just have a fondness for him—she was passionately, obsessively in love with him. She'd write him letters in which she'd say, "Oh, I can't wait to be in your arms ..." Now, beautiful women chase pastors too, but this one happened to be an extremely homely woman, and was also older than Chuck. And she was terribly jealous of me. She'd sit directly across from me in church and stare holes through me. Apparently, she had dabbled in witchcraft and her husband once heard her chant, "Die, Kay, die." We knew because he called Chuck to tell him about it.

I prayed for her week after week after week. And she continued to swoon over Chuck and stare holes through me. People who weren't even aware of the situation would come to me and say, "Kay, there's a woman over there who keeps staring at you." She really had such a strong demonic spirit that even when I hadn't yet spotted her across the sanctuary, I could feel her fixation upon me.

One morning as I got up out of bed, my back immediately got a catch in it. I thought, *Oh dear, what now?* I went to brush my teeth and I was suddenly overwhelmed by an awful headache. As I climbed into the bathtub, I felt shooting pains in my stomach. And I thought, *This is too much for one Monday morning.*

So I began to pray, "Lord, what is going on?" And just like that, the face of this woman came before me. I said, "Oh, it's her, Lord, isn't it?" Just as plain as anything, I knew she was using her witchcraft against me. I prayed, "I refuse it in the name of the Lord Jesus Christ. I stand on the authority given to Your disciples in Luke 10:19. She is a defeated foe and that is that." Instantly, the headache began to go, and when I got out of the tub, I stood straight up without a stomachache. But when I looked into the mirror, I was as pale as a ghost.

I had a lunch appointment with two friends at noon. When I arrived at the restaurant and sat down, one of my friends looked at me and questioned, "Are you all right?"

I replied, "No."

"What's the matter?" she asked.

I paused for a minute, but then I said, "Would you believe … witchcraft?" I thought she would laugh at that.

But she didn't. My two friends looked at each other and said, "There's something we need to tell you."

They then went on to tell me that the woman who was crazy for Chuck had gone to another woman at our Bible study that very morning, and declared that her husband would be dead by Thanksgiving and I would be dead by Christmas.

When I left that lunch, I went straight to Chuck and I told him everything. Chuck's assistant, Romaine, was there too and he said, "I'll take care of that." Chuck wrote a letter at once to the woman stating, "Even if my wife died, I wouldn't be interested in you." That was a comfort.

The following Thursday was Thanksgiving, so I had a whole houseful of company that came with me to the Thanksgiving service on Wednesday night. When we arrived, I walked into the sanctuary to sit where I always sit. Romaine warned me, "Lady, don't go in there. She's here again tonight. But I promise you, she won't be again."

But I had been praying with my two intercessory friends all that week, and we had been agreeing together and standing in the power of the Lord. I said, "Romaine, the victory is so strong in my life tonight. She could sit there and do anything she wanted but she can't touch me. I know she has been defeated." And I did know. For the entire service, I was so uplifted in thanksgiving and praise, I wasn't even aware of her presence. It was as if she wasn't even there. And after that night, she never showed up again.

God is your victory. When people come in to your church who are bent on destruction, trust in the Lord, keep your heart steadfast and set on Him, and watch Him deliver you. Many times you don't have to do anything at all—He does the work for you. He doesn't want people in the church disrupting your fellowship. He'll take care of it, one way or another.

As the handmaiden of the Lord, we are required to do His work—to love the people, bless the people, feed the people, and minister to the needs of the people. And there's a verse for the handmaiden of God—a special promise that will carry you through the difficult moments.

First Corinthians 15:58 tells us, "Therefore, my beloved brethren, be steadfast, immovable, always abounding in the work of the Lord, knowing that your labor is not in vain in the Lord." Isn't that beautiful? However, we need to pay close attention to that phrase, "in the Lord." Whatever work we do must be "in the Lord."

The labor we do outside of the Lord might appear as if it profits a lot here on earth, but it won't last eternally. No matter how good or how wonderful it is, it won't last. It will just be wood, hay and stubble. But the work we do *in the Lord* is not wood, hay and stubble—it's gold and silver and precious stones.

As a pastor's wife, it is vital to check yourself and make sure that your labor is *in the Lord*. I sometimes meet women who are busy beyond all reasonable sense, and I have to wonder if their labor is truly in the Lord. I don't mean that these women are busy in the ordinary sense. We all have times when everything comes upon us seemingly at once and we barely have time to catch our breath. I'm talking about *crazy* busyness. The woman who is unreasonably busy is running here and she's dashing there, and it happens week after week after week. She'll say, "Oh, I've got so much to do! I'm so exhausted!" I believe if she sat down before the Lord with her "to do" list, He'd say, "You can eliminate this, and this ... and this."

One way to determine whether or not your labor is in the Lord is to check your motivation. Why are you doing all these things? Who called you to do it? Who are you doing it for?

Before I ever ask a woman to be on a planning committee at Calvary, or even for the pastors' wives retreat, I make sure I know her. There are women in every fellowship who desire the chance to get up to speak only to be seen by people. That's their one and only motivation. We don't like to think that, but it's true. When they get up to speak, it's rarely very effective. It's not much of an influence, because the motivation of their heart is wrong.

But a pastor's wife can have that same motivation. She can get busy just to be seen by people. Or she might have such a desperate need for people's approval that she works herself half to death, simply to receive the response from others saying, "Oh, look at what a wonderful pastor's wife she is." Forget that. The only approval you need is God's approval. We can wrongly think that people will respect us only if we keep constantly busy. But I have found that no matter how small or how large a church, the people will respect me only as I am able to respect myself enough to say no to certain things. "I can do this, but I'm sorry, I cannot do that." People respect you when you stand strongly in love for what you can and cannot do.

Now, there will always be those who ask you to do more than is reasonable, and they'll use guilt to motivate you. They'll ask you to teach a Bible study even though the Lord may not have called you to do it. They'll push you right in to it. And you will tremble and shake all night and you won't be able to sleep. You'll be yelling at the children and acting cranky toward your husband because he went into the ministry in the first place—all because you allowed someone to push you into a ministry where God did not call you.

Maybe you are not motivated by the expectations others place on you, but you are prompted by the unmet needs within you. A lot of us have unmet needs and we can take on a work that we think is pleasing unto the Lord just to satisfy those needs. But if that's your driving force, you will not be very effective in that ministry and you will easily burn out. At the very least, you will be frustrated. You will never find the

satisfaction you're looking for in trying to do a work you've not been empowered by the Holy Spirit to do.

Sometimes women are motivated by competition. They look at someone else doing a work and say, "If she can do it, I can do it." Sometimes people will feel competitive over a particular gift of the Spirit. We've seen women who only want one gift, and that's the ability to give a word of knowledge. I think they wanted others to look at them and say, "Oh, she knows things! Isn't that glorious?" They don't realize that a lot of time is spent in intercession for that person whom God had given them a word of knowledge. Along with the word of knowledge one must have a very strong intercessory prayer life.

Another proof that we are laboring in the flesh, and not in the Lord, is we eventually become miffed or aggravated if our ideas aren't accepted or we aren't complimented for what we do. The handmaiden of the Lord understands humility. She isn't upset when things don't go her way— instead she endures with gladness. She's not running around constantly looking for compliments or approval. Now, God will nudge somebody to come up and encourage you by saying, "That really blessed me." Or you get letters. We all love that. We need it and we appreciate it. But that is not the motivation for doing the Lord's work.

If you're not sure of what your ministry should be in the church, begin to pray. Ask God what He wants you to do and allow Him to show you. But don't expect a burning bush or a loud cymbal or a great light to appear over your head. The Lord is more likely to reveal your ministry to you in a very natural way. You'll feel drawn to a particular need. It will be comfortable for you … or then again, maybe it won't. Sometimes the desire burns in your heart to do a certain work, but it's a stretch for you because it requires you to do something out of your comfort zone.

Maybe you're not used to speaking in front of others, or praying out loud, and this work will require that. Be willing to be stretched.

Now, the other extreme is the woman who says no to everything, except the one ministry she considers her own. You may have one main ministry in the church, but as the pastor's wife—and more importantly, as the handmaiden of the Lord—you have to be open to doing all sorts of smaller things that come along. Again, you need balance, wisdom and direction from the Lord in order to know when to say yes and when to say no.

You know those cleaning ladies who come in and say, "I don't wash windows, I don't change beds and I don't do laundry." Some pastors' wives can have that same attitude which tells the people, "Don't expect me to do this and don't expect me to do that." The point I'm making here may seem contrary to what I said earlier, but there's a vast difference between saying no to something because you don't feel the Lord is calling you to do it, and saying no to something because it's not your favorite thing or it's an inconvenience to you.

I had an acquaintance whose husband pastored a denominational church of about 250 people. Someone called her one day needing information. She said, "We simply do not have time to find that out for you. We are busy doing much bigger things!" She told me about that conversation and was really complaining about the nerve of some people.

I said, "You know, I want to tell you something. Chuck has three services on Sunday morning. At each of those services, there's a minimum of 3,000 people in the sanctuary, and more in the overflow halls, plus hundreds of children in the Sunday school. All together, there are probably about 4,000 people on the premises each service."

Then I said, "After church one Sunday a woman came into the office and said that she had lost her earring. It wasn't big—just a tiny gold earring. Chuck overheard and said, 'Show me where you were sitting.' She led us back to her seat, and there we all went—down on hands and knees crawling around through that crazy shag carpet trying to find her gold earring."

I then told this acquaintance, "It's so important that you don't tell people, 'I'm too busy. What I'm doing is so much bigger and greater.'" If you can't do it, if you're too weary or you haven't the time, be honest. But don't say, "I don't wash windows and I don't change beds and I don't do laundry."

A servant of Jesus Christ does what is at hand if it is in her power to do it—and she does it with gladness. I personally believe that one of the responsibilities of the pastor's wife is to notice whether the church is clean or not. If it isn't, and you don't have a custodian, see if you can get a group of women to help you wash the windows, wipe down the windowsills and spiffy up the church a bit.

One Sunday night I went into the women's restroom and noticed that someone had used soap to write all over the mirror. It was smeared from one end to the other. While I was in there I saw woman after woman walk in, look at the mirror, and walk right out. Now, I don't tell you this to show you what a humble servant I am, but just to make the point about doing the task that is in front of you. It didn't take but a minute to wet some paper towels and wash it off. While I was doing so, my friend, Carol, came in and saw what I was doing. She said, "Oh my goodness," and grabbed some paper towels and helped me finish.

What do you see when you walk into your church? If there's tissue on the floor when you go into your restroom, pick it up and dispose of it.

Don't say, "Those janitors, why aren't they doing their job?" or "These people, what slobs they are." Just pick it up and throw it away. It doesn't matter who does it. When you're the handmaiden of the Lord, you're ready for those little unexpected jobs—and you do it with a happy attitude.

What we need is balance. Don't be like Wonder Woman who suddenly drops from the sky with her beautiful armor and her gorgeous figure, and *Zap!* Everything is fixed. That's not your job as the pastor's wife. Your job is to wait on the Lord and complete the task He asks you to do. Your job is to obey Colossians 3:17, which tells us, "Whatever you do in word or deed, do all in the name of the Lord Jesus," and Colossians 3:23, "And whatever you do, do it heartily, as to the Lord and not to men." Do it how? Heartily, meaning "with all your heart." If you pick up a dropped tissue, if you clean a windowsill, if you prepare a luncheon—do it with all your heart. If you're in the kitchen doing the dishes after a fellowship, don't just do the dishes. Check the refrigerator too and if it needs cleaning, wash it out. Do it heartily unto the Lord with joy. Make it enjoyable. Laugh with your women, and teach them that they can enjoy Jesus while they're doing even the smallest jobs. Proverbs 17:22 says, "A merry heart does good, like medicine." Sometimes the women come in hurting and crushed in spirit. Let that merry heart of yours be contagious. Now, don't be a laughing fool, but bless them with a joyful spirit.

There's nothing like working for the Lord. If you work for men, you'll be disappointed. You might think you've written the most powerful teaching ever, so you call your friend over to validate it. But on that particular day your friend had too much coffee and she's a nervous, shaky wreck. Even though you give out hints here and there as you're reciting your great teaching, she doesn't catch a single one. Just about

the time you're ready to hit your most powerful point, she runs out of steam, nods off and misses it altogether. You're dashed to the ground because you didn't get the approval of men. It's so much better to do everything as unto the Lord.

Not only does God see every tiny act of service you do for Him, He rewards you for each one. Colossians 3:24 continues on to say, "Knowing that from the Lord you will receive the reward of the inheritance." There's a reward waiting for you for all those things you endure with gladness now.

Many times when I was teaching our Joyful Life class, my alarm would go off at 5:30 on Friday morning and I would groan. I felt such weariness in my flesh. But then I'd remember that God was watching. The knowledge that the Lord sees me and is pleased by my service helped me to spring out of bed. Hardly a Friday went by that God didn't give me that awareness. Not a single work I do for Him—or that you do for Him—will go unnoticed or unrewarded.

I want to end this chapter with that thought: God sees. Do you know that today? Do you really know it? God sees. And when we put aside our plans and our will to please Him, it is never in vain. Let that thought sink in, because if you don't have a heavenly perspective of what you're doing here on earth, you're going to have a lot of fleshly reactions to situations that come into your life. You'll question, "Why do I have to do it? Why doesn't somebody else do it? Why doesn't God raise up these people? Why?"

But when you think eternally instead of temporally, you can endure the unexpected with gladness. Instead of complaining, you'll say, "There's nobody to teach that Sunday school class this morning, so I will teach it. It's not my ministry, but as a servant of the Lord, I can teach class today." God knows you really wanted to be in the sanctuary that morning to hear your husband preach. But He also knows that the time you will spend teaching those precious little ones will not be in vain. You're not just a fill-in that day. No. It mattered to our Lord. And you never know what He was up to. You're liable to have one of those children come back some day and say, "Do you remember that one Sunday, fifteen years ago? That was the only Sunday I remember you taking our class, but you said something that day that changed the whole course of my life."

Things like that happen when we are servants, handmaidens of the Lord Jesus Christ.

Chapter Five

ON THE ALTAR

J'VE BEEN thinking a lot about choices and how greatly a life can be altered because of one little choice. If you've never really thought about the impact a single choice can make, just look at the garden of Eden. The first ever recorded choice made by a woman was there in the garden—by Eve. What a disaster that decision brought upon all of us.

Satan did to Eve what he tries to do to each one of us today. He deceived her into doubting God's word. He asked Eve in Genesis 3:1, "Hath God said …?" In other words, "Did God *really* say if you ate of the fruit of that tree you'd die? Now look, Eve, you and I know that won't happen. I mean, He created you to be in this garden. He created you for Himself. You know you're not going to die." Even though God had spoken clearly to Eve, she allowed the enemy to cast doubt on His words.

I once knew a beautiful girl who walked with Jesus in a manner that used to inspire everyone. She was a light and a wonder to all who knew her. But some tragic circumstances came up in her life and Satan saw an open opportunity. He began to work on her, just like he worked on Eve. "How could God let you go through this? Why is He allowing this to happen? That's so unfair, so unjust. He could have rescued you, but He didn't."

She listened to those lies, believed them, and then she turned to the world. Of course, the further away she walked from God, the worse she felt. Eventually, she became so emotionally distraught she had to be hospitalized. It's very sad when a Christian believes the lies of Satan.

There's only one antidote which works against Satan's lies, and that's the devoted life. Only a life completely committed to the Lord Jesus Christ will defeat the enemy when he whispers, "Has God really said …?"

So what is the devoted life? It is a sacrifice that is never taken back. In Leviticus 27:28 the Lord writes,

> No devoted offering that a man may devote to the LORD of all that he has, both man and beast, or the field of his possession, shall be sold or redeemed; every devoted offering is most holy to the LORD.

This literally means that if you brought a sacrifice to the temple and you gave it to the priest to place upon the altar, you could never take that sacrifice back. If you offered a person to the Lord—as Hannah did with her son, Samuel—they become a holy thing, set apart exclusively for God's use. That is the devoted life: You are set apart exclusively for God's use. Your life is no more your own than Samuel's was. Your life is completely God's. He is not just Lord of your life—you are completely His.

The obvious question then is, how do I become devoted to Him? There is a verse so familiar we sometimes gloss right over the truth it contains. Romans 12:1 states:

> I beseech you therefore, brethren, by the mercies of God, that you present your bodies a living sacrifice, holy, acceptable to God, which is your reasonable service.

That's how we become devoted to God. A shallow consecration will never stand. When the flames get hot and the trials get hard, those who made an emotional dedication will just hop off the altar again. Their offering is not complete. It wasn't based on devotion, but just on emotion. The only consecration that will endure the hard times is a complete, absolute, unreserved, irretrievable offering.

A good example of this kind of devotion is the marriage commitment. In this day and age, people don't like commitments. That's because we live in a society where it's perfectly acceptable to marry over and over again. So the word "commitment" has gone out the window. But not for Christians.

I once knew a man who had been married forty-five years. He had been a good-looking man in his youth and he was one of those men who aged handsomely. In all the years of his marriage, there had never been a taint of infidelity, despite the fact that he was constantly surrounded by lovely, available women. Someone once asked him, "How have you stayed faithful to your wife all these years despite so many temptations?"

He said, "The day I married my wife I made a commitment, and I've never allowed my mind or my heart to think any other way. I've never thought of divorce. I've never entertained the thought of any alliance with another woman. I have always put my wife first in my heart—right after the Lord."

Another friend of mine gave his wife a bracelet on their wedding day. It was inscribed, "One life, one love." That describes the devoted life. One life, one love.

Is that how you feel about the Lord Jesus Christ? Is He the love of your life—above your husband, your family, your career, and your desires? It's so important to make Him your greatest love. Unless you are completely committed to Him, you will not make choices consistent with the Christian life. And without complete devotion, you will not be the witness you could be for Him and you will never be an influence to others for the kingdom.

On the other hand, once you do make that commitment, then your choices and decisions will line up accordingly. All your thoughts, your desires, your words and your actions will line up according to God's pleasure. Do we fail? Oh yes. We fail and we sin and we fall short. There's forgiveness for all of that. Sometimes we take a little detour here and there, but we get right back on the path. We ask for forgiveness and cleansing, because our desire is to please Him. When we're living the devoted life, the world no longer has any pull on us. That's because there's no room for Satan in the devoted heart.

I remember many years ago when my granddaughter, Kristyn, was at our house. She was just a tiny thing, and she was being a little naughty with me. She was an absolute living doll, but she did have those misbehaving moments now and then. And on this particular day, she decided to throw my house slipper at me.

I looked at her and said, "Kristyn, you may not throw slippers at Grandma. That just isn't done."

She repented quickly. "Sor-ry."

I said, "When you do things like that, you could get little black spots on your pure white heart that loves Jesus so much." Then I said, "You don't want a polka-dotted heart, do you?"

She laughed and played right along with it. "Sor-ry," she said again. She wanted instant cleansing so she didn't get a polka-dotted heart.

We don't want a polka-dotted heart either, do we? We want hearts that are purely devoted to God and deaf to the lies of the enemy. Oh, how Satan works to ensnare us! "Has God really said …?" The heart that is fully committed to God knows Him too well to doubt Him. The devoted heart recognizes Satan's lies quickly.

When I went to visit the hospitalized woman I mentioned earlier, she said, "You know, Kay, I wonder if one of my problems is that I need to forgive God."

Forgive God—God, who has never sinned? God, who is pure, holy and righteous? *We* need to forgive God? Never! Only a person living an uncommitted, undevoted life could ever believe such a lie.

As a pastor's wife, it is very important to study the Word to find out who God is and what He's really like. You should never utter the statement: "I'm angry with God." How could you be angry with a God who loves you so dearly that He gave His only begotten Son to die for you? How could you be angry with a God who has never had a trace of iniquity in Him, but who is all righteousness, justice and truth? Oh, beloved, don't ever say it. And don't allow others you care for to say it, either. But if they do, don't bark at them, be gentle and teach them.

When this woman made that statement to me, I responded, "You know, God loves you, and He wouldn't do anything that was wrong for you." Then I talked to her about the character of God and about His incomparable goodness. "God has not brought this trouble into your life—it's Satan. Don't you see that? We're living in a world where Satan is the prince of the power of the air."

After a while, she said, "Oh." That was it—just "Oh." But it was a start. I prayed that she would come to that place of devotion and would finally place her life on the altar of sacrifice.

God desires us to come to that place of devotion. We can hear His heart's cry in Jeremiah 30:21. Though He's speaking about leadership in this passage, the desire of His heart is clear: Who will devote himself to be close to Me?

> "Their leader will be one of their own; their ruler will arise from among them. I will bring him near and he will come close to Me, for who is he who will devote himself to be close to Me?" declares the Lord (*NIV*).

Don't you want to be a woman who answers that cry? Don't you want to say, "I will do it, Lord. I want to be close to You. I will put my life on the altar"?

This is not just some romantic ideal. God is not asking you to be like Mother Teresa or Joan of Arc. So often when somebody hears the message to present their body as a living sacrifice, they get these grand notions and say, "Yes, I will go to the mission field and die for the Lord. I will drink native poison or be boiled in a cauldron. I will. I will do it." But do you know what happens to that kind of rash, romantic offering? It's just a flame that spurts up and quickly dies, because it's only a shallow consecration. It's not a fully surrendered offering that has first counted the cost.

"But, Kay, I'm a pastor's wife. Of course I've given my life to Him as a living sacrifice. Boy, if you lived in our parsonage for a week, you'd know it's a living sacrifice." That's not what I'm talking about. I'm talking about giving your life unto God and into His control.

Elisabeth Elliot once shared a poll taken by a Christian magazine. They surveyed a great number of pastors' wives from all over the nation asking them to list the three subjects they would most like to read about. What three subjects would you have chosen? The answer to that tells a lot about you and what you're thinking about the ministry. According to this poll, the number one answer was "inspirational reading." Elisabeth commented, "That's a feeble term for a pastor's wife to use, really."

The second subject was "loneliness," and the third was "self-image." Elisabeth added, "When the second concern of ministers' wives is loneliness, and the third is self-image, we're really in trouble." She then shared about how ungodly the whole notion of self-image is, saying, "People think if I have good self-esteem, nothing bad will ever happen to me again. We think we'll never have problems or be rejected if we can just improve our self-esteem."

The Word does not teach this at all. Jesus never taught the disciples to have self-confidence, did He? Can you find it in the Bible? No, because Jesus never taught that. And Jesus never taught that we were to have faith in ourselves. Is there a Scripture anyplace that reads, "Have faith in yourself"? Who are we to have faith in? We're to have faith in God—not in ourselves.

Concerning loneliness, Elisabeth said she'd always accepted it as part of the price of being a minister's wife. It is important that you hear this. I have heard so many complaints from pastors' wives about their

loneliness until I simply cannot stand hearing it anymore. Loneliness is part of the price. Oftentimes your husband has to be with other people.

Occasionally I would say, "Chuck, may we leave the phone off the hook for ten minutes during dinner?" Sometimes he said yes and sometimes he said no. Now, that is the kind of commitment Chuck has to his calling. Never, in all the years of his ministry, has he taken two days off a week. Never. Now, your husband may not be able to go at Chuck's pace—he has energy beyond anything I've ever seen—and I'm not saying it's wrong to take two days off in a week.

What I want to share with you is commitment. And today, you need to realize that you've been chosen by God just as much as your husband. You've been given a high calling and a privilege. "He who finds a wife finds a good thing, and obtains favor from God" (Proverbs 18:22). When your husband chose to marry you, he obtained favor from God. You are chosen. But loneliness is part of this calling.

I know women whose husbands are in entirely different occupations and their husbands are gone much more than Chuck—and he's gone quite a bit. But when you gripe, moan and complain about loneliness, you only make your husband miserable. You hinder him. He cannot do the work of the Lord the way he should. A woman whose life is on the altar of sacrifice, however, does not complain about loneliness.

Now, I do believe it is within our place to say, "Hey, I miss you. Could we find a time to be together?" I hope he's a man who says, "Of course." But if he isn't—if he's a husband who is truly neglecting you—then the best place for you to do business about that is on your knees.

I have never changed one thing about Chuck. I can't change the way he dresses. I can't change the way he sometimes mispronounces words.

In fact, I've given up. I have found I mispronounce them too. Really, it's kind of endearing that they make mistakes too. We all do. That's comforting.

But don't complain about loneliness. We have been seduced into thinking that loneliness is a problem which must be solved. Everyone is lonely at times. Every single person—not just pastors' wives. You can even be lonely while you're with the one you love. Loneliness is just a part of our walk, but it can also serve a beautiful purpose.

When Chuck was away on a trip, there was no one to cook for but myself, and oh, how I wished I could have Chuck there. But I still had Jesus with me. I wasn't really alone. I would get in the car and I'd say, "Lord Jesus, we're going to the market now."

A few years after Elisabeth Elliot's husband was killed by the Auca Indians, she went back with her three-year-old daughter as a missionary to those same people. She lived for weeks without any contact whatsoever except with the Indians and her little three-year-old. She commented, "There were weeks that went by when I didn't hear any English other than what my little girl said." You think you're lonely? Elisabeth's husband had been killed by the same people she was ministering to, and yet she went back to those people. Is her life on the altar? Oh, yes. When you think about what it had cost her, it makes you feel like your consecration has not been very pronounced, doesn't it?

Hearing this warning about loneliness is enough to make some pastors' wives jump right off the altar of sacrifice. "Kay, this isn't the life for me. I'm not content to be by myself." Well, you need to learn to be content, or you will not survive this life. This really is a glorious life! When we're totally devoted to Him, our attitude will be one of absolute obedience.

Instead of taking orders from some slimy serpent, we'll get our orders from the King Himself.

Consider now an area that will test your devotion to Him. You may think, *Well, I've been on that altar of sacrifice. I believe I really have. I sincerely think I'm committed.* I want to give you three principles. The first is found in Matthew 16:24.

> If anyone desires to come after Me, let him deny himself, and take up his cross, and follow Me.

Deny yourself. Oh, how we hate to hear that. Only the devoted child of God can do it. You have to be dead to yourself to really deny yourself.

In his book, *The Jesus Style,* [5] Gayle Erwin said there's a condensed secret found in the Bible, and that is: Deny yourself. All the principles of the Word of God fall into place when we put this one Scripture into effect. But you cannot do this unless your life has been put on the altar of sacrifice and the flames are burning out your self life.

Self-denial is not natural to any of us. It has to be supernatural. Most of us know how difficult diets are. None of us like to go on a diet. If you want to know how great your willpower is, just go on a diet. The self hates being denied, and we live in a culture that says, "Do not deny yourself—just please yourself."

If you really want to know the conflict of the culture, move to Newport Beach. There are Newport Beach women who weigh ninety-eight pounds and live to please themselves. Now, how they do it, I will never know. I've never tapped into their secret, except that their vanity must be so great that they starve themselves to death. I don't know how they do it, but the world says, "Please yourself. Please yourself."

Very often, the refusal to deny self and the insistence to please self has devastating consequences on those around us. The lady we bought our home from said, "I have to sell." In fact, she sold it to us at a ridiculously low price. She stated, "I hate to tell you this, but my husband and I have just separated. We became a part of that Newport Beach crowd and he's had one affair after another. My husband's into womanizing and I just couldn't take it any longer." This is what the world says, "Please yourself." She had four children—two on drugs. It was a mess. An absolute mess. "Please yourself." That's what the world says.

The Word of God says, "Deny yourself." And interestingly enough, it is one of the most wonderful principles for joy. You know the days when you successfully diet, and you go to bed that night and you may be hungry, but aren't you happy? I am. The few times I've done it and stayed away from that marvelous chocolate, I have felt so good about it. I thought, *Oh, I'll do this tomorrow too.* Dieting does not come easily for any of us. Because of our flesh, denial does not come easy. Our flesh constantly screams, "Please me. Please me." We are selfish.

Chuck Jr. said he was in a bookstore section previewing book titles, *Self Esteem: Understanding Yourself; Self Actualization; Self Love; Learn to Love Yourself;* and *Self Awareness.* He said, "Mom, guess what? They were all under the heading of 'Self Help.'" I don't think the self needs any help, do you? I think the only way to deal with self is to put it on the altar once and for all.

A friend once gave me a book called, *Please Understand Me ...* a book which was supposed to help me understand myself. She knows I have a morbid interest in some of that stuff. There was a test in the front of the book asking seventy questions and giving only two choices to answer each question.

Now, I am terrible at these tests. One of the questions was, "Would you rather have a boss that is fair or kind?" Well, I want a boss that's both. So, how do I make a choice? I was analyzing all of this, and making a mountain out of a molehill. So I just answered, "Fair." I thought, *Oh, I'm just going to get through this test.* Then the next question was, "Which do you not admire most in a person, injustice or mercilessness?" Oh, boy, I don't know. The whole test was like that. After completing the test, your answers determine what occupation best suits you. You'll never guess what I should be ... a mortician. Isn't that great? I think I made a wrong choice somewhere. Do you understand why I'm so interested in the choices you make?

Jesus said if you want to be His disciple, you need to deny yourself. If you have not put your life on the altar of sacrifice and you are not walking in self-denial, then you're not His disciple. That's not Kay's idea, that's what the Word teaches us. Deny yourself what? Anything that would stop you from growing in Him—His beauty, His likeness, His glory, His greatness, His compassion, His purity. Stop indulging in self-pity. Stop indulging in the flesh or any area that would grieve the heart of God or stumble others.

You know, what we are inside is communicated to others unconsciously. For instance, if I were involved in a torrid affair—at my age, this isn't a problem, believe me. At any age this should not be a problem, as long as your life is on the altar of sacrifice—but if I were to be involved in something like that, it wouldn't matter how many wonderful, righteous, holy things I said to the people in my church. That spirit of self-indulgence, that place of Satan in my life, would go forth, and the people in my congregation would pick up on that spirit of lust. We produce the fruit of what we are and there's no hiding it.

Do you think you can walk into church on Sunday morning and flirt with some guy in the congregation and still have the people think, *There's our pious, wonderful, precious pastor's wife*? No! Instead, people in your congregation will pick up on your spirit. Pretty soon, a marriage in your church breaks up. He's found someone else, or she decides she doesn't love him anymore. Then a young, single woman starts sleeping around. It happens. When you don't deny yourself for the Lord Jesus Christ and instead live for your own selfish pleasure, you will contaminate the people God has entrusted to you. I've seen it happen over and over again.

If, as a pastor's wife, you are involved in anything immoral—even if it's just in your mind—it proves that your life is not on the altar of sacrifice and you're not wholly devoted to God. Now, that's a tough thing to say, but God has revealed to me that I must say it. All over the country, churches are in chaos right now because either the pastor or the pastor's wife has indulged in that sort of thing.

Oh, beloved, I'm pouring out my heart—and I know my heart is on target with His. It is really God who is pleading with you. You may already know how important it is to deny yourself and live for Jesus. But I'm fast after those who are not, because you can do so much harm in the body. I can't bear to hear of one more pastor's wife who has run off with somebody. Don't you dare. Boy, this is Mama Kay at her toughest, isn't it? It's time for us to behave ourselves and walk as women of God.

You must deny yourself. You must take up your cross. And what does it mean to take up your cross? It means laying down your will to do God's will. That's the simplest definition I know. Lay down your will to do His will. Deny yourself.

The Privilege

Ruth Bell Graham wrote that after her husband, Billy, became so famous, she became aware that the world was watching every penny she spent. She knew that she had to refrain from indulging herself in jewelry or expensive clothing. And yet, she had to sit with presidents and heads of state and even the Queen of England. But she chose to dress in a way in which the world couldn't find fault. She never wanted anyone to say, "She's spending the tithe money on herself."

Once Ruth was handed a thousand-dollar honorarium for a speaking engagement. She designated it to be sent to a certain orphanage. Well, the people sent the money to the orphanage, but they also sent her a thousand-dollar gift certificate to Neiman Marcus. So she went to Neiman Marcus, bought a thousand-dollar gold bracelet and gave it to a Christian relief organization—with the stipulation that they sell it for twice its value and give the money for missions work. That's where her heart was.

Beloved, learn to deny yourself. Don't be the fashion plate of the church. You don't have to dress shabbily, but don't overindulge yourself with fashion. There's a place right in between. And don't always be concerned with becoming thin. It sets a bad example to your congregation and puts too much emphasis on that sort of thing. Now, I do believe in keeping fit and staying healthy, but I don't believe in making weight loss the biggest goal in your life. You're not the pastor's wife because you have the most admirable figure.

It really comes down to this one question: Are you willing to deny yourself so that your husband's ministry can be more effective to the people of your church? What about in the simple things, like how you answer the telephone? I know I've talked about those phone calls a great deal, but that's because it's such a constant test for me. I have days where I really, really have to work on my tone so that I don't answer "Hello?" in a way which lets the person on the other end of the line know that I'm just about to run out the door, I'm already ten minutes late, and I simply don't have time for their call. God is teaching me, "Kay, be gentle on the phone. Be loving. Be sweet—even if you don't have the time. Deny your own reactions."

The second principle of the devoted life is found in John 15:13.

> Greater love has no one than this, than to lay down one's life for his friends.

Again, I think we misinterpret those words and we imagine some great heroic deed. We see ourselves doing a spectacular act like jumping in front of a bus to save a toddler. We think, *Oh, greater love is laying down my life*. It's dying to yourself and living for Jesus. Many times I think it might be easier to die for Him than to really live for Him the way we ought to. Greater love has no woman, no pastor's wife, than this: that she lay down her life for her husband, for her children, and for her congregation.

We have dozens of opportunities every single day to lay down our lives for another. For example, one day I walked out the door at the conference center and tripped over the mat, which was kind of rumpled up. I almost fell down and I really wanted to kick the mat. You know how you get that frustrated reaction. I kept walking, but then the thought came into my mind, *What if somebody else came out that door and stumbled?* So I went back and put that mat down the way it belonged. You know, that isn't much of an illustration. It's such a little thing. But it is a picture of what a pastor's wife should be doing. You should be straightening out the mat so other people won't stumble.

Go back. Do the thing that helps them continue along the path. Get the rocks out of the way. Go before them and even remove the pebbles that might get trapped in their shoes, and do those things that will make their walk with Jesus easier. Lay down your life for them. Care for your congregation. Love them with a tender love that is willing to counsel them and take time with them.

How about laying your life down in prayer time? Dr. Alan Redpath said—and I thought it was a wonderful thing for a seventy-eight-year-old man to say—"Prayer time is not easy." It doesn't matter what age you are. We have a notion that some people are born to be intercessors. They wake up early, get out of bed and just cannot help themselves. Every day they drop to their knees and they stay there for six hours. And, of course, you could never be one of them. Well, I couldn't either. So the temptation is to lay aside our prayer life. We think, *Prayer should be easy, and since it isn't, I will forget it.* That's not true. There have been many, many times when I have not felt like praying, but I have done it because the Lord tells me to do it. It's one of the ways we love and care for our people.

Elisabeth Elliot once said that she gets up at four o'clock every morning for prayer time. She does it because her daddy always did it. But when people hear that, they say to her, "Oh, you must be an early riser." She added, "I'm not a morning person—not at all. Actually, it's not easy; it's very difficult for me. It's cold where I live, so I have to wrap myself up in a blanket. But you know how I do it? I do what my daddy used to do. The night before, I lay out my notebook, a pencil, my Bible, and the blanket I'm going to wrap myself in, and when the alarm goes off, I get up." She concluded, "All I can say to you about a prayer life is: Do it."

And that's about all I can say to you: Do it. It's not easy, and Satan will fight you on it. I have been down on my knees when I felt nothing happening spiritually. Nothing. "God," I'll say, "You seem so far from me." But as I stay there and I stay there, oh, things begin to happen. Things happen in our church. The impossible becomes possible. People reconcile. That person who was so angry is suddenly a precious friend. That man who was an alcoholic comes to Jesus Christ. Miracles occur. I change, and Chuck changes. And glorious things happen.

Are you willing to lay down your life for your husband's ministry—for the people God has entrusted to you—in prayer? Are you willing to lay down your life so that troubled households will be filled with God's love? That the wife you're praying for will be strengthened to endure for her husband's salvation? That those kids involved in drugs will be delivered? Are you willing? God is asking you—and what He's asking isn't easy. Following Jesus has never been presented as an easy life, except by a fool. It is not an easy life. It will take everything you've got inside of you. But praise God, He empowers and enables you by His Holy Spirit to do it.

Another part of laying down your life is letting go of your rights. This can be very difficult, but many times, the only way to have peace is to let go of those rights.

My friend, Martha, is a wonderful grandmother. For a long time, she had been worried about her grandson because she felt her daughter wasn't feeding him the nutritious things he needed. He ate a lot of sugar, but he never seemed to eat any fruits or vegetables. Martha kept quiet about this for a long, long time. But one night while she was visiting, she watched her daughter hand her little grandson a Twinkie. The night had been very relaxed and comfortable, and Martha thought this might be the perfect opportunity to say something. So she did. And both her daughter and son-in-law blew up at her.

She left their house immediately and went home. She really believed that she was right and they were wrong, and the only way they would ever understand that was if she stayed away and let them have their way. She figured that eventually, her grandson would get sick and his parents would see the light. So she stayed away for several days. Until one morning, while she was in prayer, she heard the Lord say, "You are to call and tell them you're sorry."

"Sorry?" she said. "I'm not sorry. They're wrong. That child's going to be sick."

But the Lord said, "I'll take care of the child. You lay down your life to make things right."

Martha obeyed what she heard. She called her daughter and said, "I'm so sorry if I offended you. I should have kept quiet. It wasn't my place."

"Oh Mom, I'm so glad to hear from you. How are you? Why don't you come over for a visit?"

Peace. Martha was right—but when she trusted God and laid down her rights, her reward was peace with her daughter.

Are you willing, in your church, to lay down your thoughts and opinions and ideas for the sake of peace? If your life is on the altar of sacrifice, you'll be willing to do it.

Is there a woman in your church who needs supporting? Are you willing to give of your time to help her? Maybe that woman is like a tree that has been bent by the storms of adversity, so go to her and strengthen her. Your life is busy and your schedule is full, and you really don't have the time to do the strengthening. But God is asking. And because it's

God, you're obedient. You lay down your life and rescue a friend who's about to be drowned by the storms of life.

The devoted life denies itself, and she lays down her rights, and then she does one more thing: she washes another's feet. This is the third principle of the devoted life. John 13:14 tells us to do it.

> If I then, your Lord and Teacher, have washed your feet, you also ought to wash one another's feet.

Now, in our culture, the literal interpretation of that verse doesn't mean much to us. I could come over with a pail of water and a towel and wash your feet, and it wouldn't be too humbling for me—because your feet are probably pretty clean. It's really not a question of cleanliness. It's a matter of servanthood. "He that would be great among you, let him be servant of all" (Mark 10:44).

Again Gayle Erwin writes in his book, *The Jesus Style*, [6] that over every pastor's door, instead of a plaque that reads "Pastor So and So" it should say "Slave." You know what "minister" means? It means to serve. You are the servant. You are not in that church to be admired because you're wonderful and you're important. You may be one of the most important people in the church—if you are, then you should be the servant of all. You should be denying yourself. You should be giving up your rights. And you should be washing other people's feet.

Pastors' wives can be so admired and so catered to and so spoiled by a congregation that she can become a bossy authoritarian. But that's not what the pastor's wife should be. She should be the loving one. You know the one requirement that a congregation has for a pastor's wife? It's very simple: they want her love. That's it. Pastors' wives need to love, respect and serve the congregation—even in the most humble of ways.

The Privilege

Years ago, a couple from Israel came over to the United States, and we set up a little reunion for them with some of the people whom they had met on one of our tours. This couple was very dear to us, and we had been trying over the years to share Jesus with them, but they hadn't yet accepted Him as their Messiah. We all met at the church one evening and had a wonderful time visiting and catching up. In fact, we had such a fun time that by the end of the evening, the kitchen floor was so sticky that just walking across it practically pulled our shoes off. And we were going to have a men's breakfast in there the next morning.

I was out saying goodbye to everyone, and when just about everybody was gone, I went back into the kitchen for something. Do you know who was down on his hands and knees scrubbing that floor? Chuck! The janitor was out playing the piano. When he heard that Chuck was in the kitchen scrubbing the floor, he about had a heart attack. He ran into the kitchen yelling, "What is he doing?!"

Chuck, who was just scrubbing away, said, "Oh, it's fine. I don't mind." He really did a beautiful job. The floors never looked cleaner.

But do you know what that did? We had been trying over and over and over again to witness to our Israeli friends of what Jesus is like. "Oh, Jesus is the Messiah!" we'd tell them. "Isaiah speaks about Him …" We told them all about prophecy. We talked with them for hours at a time and tried everything we could think of to open their eyes to their Messiah. But it wasn't until they saw Chuck scrubbing the floor that they saw Jesus.

"Chuck Smith?" they said. They had been to our Sunday morning service. They saw thousands of people gathered there. They knew that Chuck is on the radio all over the world. Do you think a man of that stature in Israel would scrub a floor? Of course not. "Chuck Smith scrubbing a floor?" They couldn't get over it. When they left two months later, they were still talking about it. "You know," they said, "we cannot forget Chuck in the kitchen scrubbing the floor." At that time, Chuck had fourteen pastors serving under him and a large janitorial staff. Do you want Jesus to be seen in your life? Then be a servant.

Your church needs a pastor's wife with a devoted heart. You may be the single most important role model in your church. It could be you hate the fishbowl life of the ministry, and you've been feeling rebellion in your heart. If that's true, you need to repent and ask God to change your attitude. Otherwise, all you will reap will be emptiness, and you will never know the unsurpassing joy and blessing that could be yours. If you want to live a life that counts, I challenge you to become devoted to Him. That's my prayer—that you will come to the place of true devotion and lay down your whole life on the altar of sacrifice.

"O Jesus, Lord and Savior, I give myself to Thee,
For Thou, in Thine atonement, didst give Thyself for me.
I own no other Master, my heart shall be Thy throne.
My life I give, henceforth to live, O Christ for Thee alone." [7]

Chapter Six

A TEACHABLE HEART

A WHILE BACK at one of our pastors' wives' retreats, we created programs with little plastic mirrors on the front. The retreat's theme was written above the mirror: "Behold the Pastor's Wife." The idea was for each woman to look at her reflection and see the handmaiden of the Lord looking back at her.

The problem with the plastic mirrors was it distorted the reflection a little bit. It didn't give a true representation of their faces. But actually that was a good illustration for our ladies, because too often we look into the wrong mirror to see who we are.

The only genuine mirror, of course, is the mirror of God's eyes. We can't see that reflection yet—that will have to wait until the moment we first

lay eyes on His face. We know from Scripture that when God looks at us, He sees His perfect, blameless daughter—spotless and beautiful through Jesus Christ. God sees you as perfect. Isn't that astounding? Isn't it a comfort? It certainly comforts me.

We all dislike things about ourselves; little nagging traits and flaws that we'd love to get rid of. I have them too. And sometimes I think, *Oh, I hate that about myself!* In spite of that, God doesn't declare, "I hate that about Kay." He sees me through the blood of Jesus. And because of that blood, what He beholds is flawless, unblemished, perfect, pure and lovely. Doesn't that thought catch your breath? There's no one on earth who sees us that way—only our heavenly Father.

The Bible tells us that God "rejoices over us with singing" (Zephaniah 3:17). I can hardly wait to hear God sing. I think that the sun will dissolve and the hills will melt and the seas will dry up when God opens His magnificent voice in song. And to think that we will be able to hear it! We're also told in Psalm 139:17-18 that His thoughts toward us outnumber the grains of sand in the sea. And Jeremiah 29:11 assures us that all those thoughts are good thoughts.

What kind of reaction do you have when you look in the mirror? I guess the answer can depend on the light you're in. Light makes a big difference. Some light is very flattering. I know people who put pink light bulbs in their living room lamps because it makes everybody look beautiful. Very posh restaurants often do this. When light is dim, we look great.

I remember one time when I had to catch a plane at six o'clock in the morning. We didn't have great light in our hotel room, and I woke up at four o'clock and applied my makeup kind of quickly and haphazardly. It didn't look bad to me at first, but once we boarded the plane and the sun came up, I got out my compact to freshen up a bit and I gasped at my reflection. It's strange how all that bright light streaming through the plane windows can wrinkle your skin in such a short time.

Harsh lighting brings out every freckle, pore and broken capillary. Really bright light can be a shock to your system, especially at my age. You look at all those glaring flaws and you feel like you could easily win the Ugly Woman of the Year award. I remember once when my delightful friend, Marge Caldwell, was speaking to our ladies. She was seventy years old at the time and she said, "I'm so old that some of the people at my church think Sarah was my best friend." That's how I feel when the lighting is bad. That's when I wish veils were back in style.

When I was a little girl, it wasn't uncommon to see a woman wearing a veil. If she wanted to cover up, she'd attach a veil to her hat. It was a wonderful thing. Not only are your flaws invisible under a veil, but you also manage to look pretty glamorous. But we just don't do that today. So we have to hope for good lighting.

Light isn't the only thing that can cause an untrustworthy reflection. The mirror itself can be the problem. A distorted mirror will not give a true reflection. We've probably all been in a fun house at an amusement park and looked at our reflection in those curved mirrors. It's good for a laugh. Suddenly, you're ten feet tall or short and squatty, weighing 3,000 pounds. We know the mirror is distorted, so we don't worry about what we see there.

A distorted mirror never reveals the whole truth, so when we look into it, we blame our flaws on the mirror itself—even if there's some truth to the flaws we see there. *Oh, this can't be me. It's this crazy mirror with those funny-looking, wavy lines running through it. There's nothing wrong with me. I'm fine.* The flesh loves a distorted mirror. Other people are like a distorted mirror. They either flatter us excessively or they criticize us unmercifully. You can't always trust the reflection you receive from other people.

Sometimes people give you the funniest compliments. Many years ago while Chuck was pastoring in a denominational church, we went to a pastors' conference together. When I saw a woman I knew, she came up to me and said, "I like that suit." For a split second, I felt pretty good. But then she added, "I liked it last year when you wore it too."

I laughed. It was pretty funny. And if you know me, you know that I don't really care about that sort of thing. If I enjoy a particular outfit, you're likely to see me wearing it for the next ten years or until it just about falls apart. Still, I thought about how that woman's comment had gone from a compliment to a criticism in just a few seconds. We can't always trust what people say to us, can we?

The only way to genuinely see your reflection is to look into the One true mirror and to bathe in His light. Second Corinthians 3:18 tells us that Jesus is the One we're to be gazing upon. "But we, beholding in a mirror the glory of the Lord, are being transformed into His likeness" (*ASB*). If we stare at ourselves too long, we don't stand a chance of being transformed. On the other hand, when we gaze upon the beauty of Jesus—all the love, gentleness, kindness and justice that are within Him—we can't help but be changed. We become what we behold.

After reading a biography about Amy Carmichael, I remember shutting the book and thinking, *I want to be like Amy Carmichael.* I had the same reaction after I read about Corrie ten Boom—and even more so after I met her and got to know firsthand what a strong, beautiful woman of God she was. I have a list of about fifteen people that I want to be like. Each of them have godly character traits that challenge and inspire me.

I believe it's good to have role models and to ask God to incorporate their best qualities into your life.

But most of all, we need to look at Jesus. We need to fix our eyes on Jesus, "the author and finisher of our faith" (Hebrews 12:2). Forget all the pictures men have drawn of Him. Focus instead on the revelation of Jesus we find in the Scriptures. The more we read about Him, the more we will want to become like Him.

Isn't that always the way it works? When I read cookbooks, I want to cook. Don't you do that? A recipe will jump out at you and you'll start imagining what it would taste like, and the next thing you know, you're at the market buying ingredients. The power of God's Word works the same way. When we gaze into the mirror of the Word and see Jesus there, we find ourselves wanting to take on His character traits. We start asking Him to change us and to mold us. We begin imitating Him. It reminds me of that old song we used to sing: "Be like Jesus, this my song, in the home and in the throng. Be like Jesus, all day long! I would be like Jesus." [8] That's the cry of my heart—and I pray it is yours too.

God's Word is a trustworthy mirror. It faithfully shows us what we are now and what we are to become. James 1:23-25 is such an important passage because it presents both the wrong and right reactions to the truth we see in the mirror of the Word.

> Anyone who listens to the Word but does not do what it says is like a man who looks at his face in a mirror and, after looking at himself, goes away and immediately forgets what he looks like. But the man who looks intently into the perfect law that gives freedom, and continues to do this, not forgetting what he has heard, but doing it—he will be blessed in what he does (*NIV*).

The commands of God speak to our hearts to show us what we ought to be. It has a transforming power like nothing else in existence. I once heard a famous psychologist declare, "Change is almost impossible in human beings." There's some truth to that—apart from God and His mighty Word. The best that psychotherapists can ever hope for is to somehow modify a person's behavior, but no human has the power to change a person. Oh, but I know Somebody who can change people, don't you? I've been changed and I'm going to be changed a lot more. And you've been changed. What you are now you will not be in years to come, because as you study Jesus, and as you look into the mirror of His Word, He transforms you into the woman you ought to be.

We can trust what we see when we ponder God's Word. Always. The reflection we see in the light of Jesus Christ is truth, and it is the *only* truth. Ephesians 5:13 says, "All things are made manifest by the light." And 1 John 1:7 reads, "If we walk in the light as He is in the light, we have fellowship with one another, and the blood of Jesus Christ His Son cleanses us from all sin." When we walk in His light, then all the darkness—every dark and ugly thing in us which causes us to strive with other people—is removed. The light of Jesus drives the darkness out. As we walk with Him, He deals one by one with all those things that keep us from being the inspiration and encouragement and influence He intends us to be to others. He erases those flaws in us that hinder our service to Him.

So what should be our reaction when the Lord begins to reveal these things to us? Well, the right reaction is James 1:25. We must be willing to receive what He reveals about ourselves and obey whatever He asks. But sometimes, we have a wrong reaction.

Instead of trusting Jesus with the flaws we see, we sink into hopeless-ness. You know that feeling when you're just about to head out the door, and you glance in the mirror and all your flaws pop out at you. Most of us feel that way at one time or another. You start thinking about how silly you look, how no one will like you, or how new people are going to take one look at you and run out of the church. We have those thoughts sometimes.

Some women will take this attitude to the extreme and exaggerate all their imperfections. "Oh, I can't do it. I can't do anything. I just can't." If one small flaw is revealed to them, then suddenly they can't do anything at all. These women are forgetting that God only uses flawed people because that's the only kind of people there are. We're all flawed—every single one of us.

Remember when God sent His angel to Gideon and told him, "Go in this might of yours, and you shall save Israel from the hand of the Midianites" (Judges 6:14). Gideon had been hiding out from his enemies and threshing wheat in secret. That's how timid Gideon was. And yet the angel called Gideon a "mighty man of valor" (verse 12). Just as God saw the potential in Gideon, He sees it in you. Don't ever let one little imperfection control your life or hinder you from the work God has called you to do. Don't crumble every time God reveals an area in you that needs work.

On the other end of the spectrum, there are people so filled with self-confidence that they love the mirror. They simply ignore or deny any revelation that doesn't suit them. "Good morning, beautiful! Not a thing needs changing. Aren't I perfect and wonderful? I'm ready. Is the world ready for me?"

These are the same people who justify all their ugly thoughts and behavior. "Sure, I'm bitter," they'll say. "But I have a right to be." They'll defend their right to be jealous, angry or unforgiving. Usually their

attitude toward God's Word on those subjects is, "I've heard all that stuff before. I don't need to hear it again." Really? I've never listened to a preacher under God's anointing and not gotten something out of his message. It didn't matter how much he might stumble through. When God's Spirit is upon him, God's truth is declared—and there's always something of value to be learned.

My heart breaks when I spot a pastor's wife with the attitude, "The world will just have to take me the way I am!" In my years of walking with the Lord, I have occasionally come across pastors' wives who have a dictatorial presence. She runs everything and she pushes people around. Sometimes her poor husband grieves over it, but she's so out of control that he doesn't dare say anything or she'll blow up at him too. The church fellowship suffers terribly. "He's a nice man," they'll say, "but his wife is impossible."

Oh, I just want to cry out from the rooftops to pastors' wives every-where: You are to be a servant to the people! You are not their boss, and they are not in the church to tend to your needs and do your bidding. Instead, you are to look at the precious people God has entrusted to you and ask, "Father, how can I serve them?" You are to help them grow and look for ways to wash their feet.

Now, unlike the woman who flatly denies she has any flaws at all, others accept the flaws that are pointed out to them. God's Word shows them where they need to make changes, and they nod and respond agreeably. "Yes. I definitely need to shape up there. I admit I'm not living up to God's purpose for me in this area." But then this person puts down the Bible, walks away, and forgets all about it.

We must be teachable. Being teachable requires two things: agreeing with what's shown to you and walking in obedience.

I used to love the story of Snow White [9] when I was a little girl. "Mirror, mirror, on the wall, who is the fairest one of all?" her wicked stepmother would say. Or "Mirror, mirror, in my hand, who is the fairest in the land?" Remember when that wicked woman looked into the mirror and it cracked? Some mornings when Chuck has asked, "How are you, Honey?" I've replied, "Well, the mirror cracked. Does that tell you anything?"

If you're reading God's Word and it's like lightning striking your heart, you'd better get down on your knees. That's evidence that God wants to do a work in you. You need to yield to that immediately, or do you know what you're liable to do? You're likely to cause harm to some Snow White out there, some precious child of God who's walking in truth and love. If you resist God's revelation, your influence on her will tear her down. The purpose for God teaching you His Word is to help you become the very best handmaiden possible.

When you open God's Word, make sure your heart is teachable. Ask Him to reveal every place in you that needs repair. You'll be blessed when you do this. This doesn't mean that every time you open the Word you will only hear, fix this, correct this or change that. Not at all. Sometimes I'll read a couple of Scriptures—especially from the Psalms—and revel in them all day long. All I can do is love and adore Him. Yet there are those days when He speaks strongly to my heart about something. He shows me what to do when the enemies come in like a flood. He reveals something in me that He wants to repair. Or He shows me a place where His grace has covered one of my flaws, and that's always so lovely to hear.

I once bought makeup at a cosmetic counter that I never ended up using. I was out shopping with some friends and we all got one. Have you ever done that? You're out with friends and you all talk each other into buying something silly? Then later you get home and you think, *What in the world am I going to do with this?* Well, we all bought this little white stick to rub under our eyes to hide any dark circles. Now, I have about as much artistic flair as a dead seal, and I am fairly certain I would end up looking like an owl if I tried to put that stuff on. Still, I liked the idea behind it. Sometimes we have flaws that need to be covered up, so God steps in and He does the covering for us. He covers us with His mercy, love and grace—and His blood. It's such a blessing when He does that for you, and people don't even seem to notice your most glaring flaws.

A few years back, Chuck was invited to speak at Forest Home, a conference center up in San Bernardino. I knew it was going to be very hot there, so I didn't pack any nylons—I just wanted to wear flip-flops. The problem was my legs were very white. Chuck is not too fond of white legs, but I just hadn't had a chance to get outside and get a tan. My daughter, Janette, said, "Mom, I've got some tanning lotion you could put on your legs." She told me she had used it herself and it was wonderful. What she forgot to tell me, though, was she'd had the stuff for five years.

We arrived at Forest Home ahead of everyone else, so I went directly to our room to apply the lotion on my legs. I was sure they'd look wonderfully tan ... but they didn't. They turned green. Green, I tell you! And I didn't have any nylons with me to cover them up. We spent the whole weekend with all these people I barely knew and I walked around looking like a frog. It was terrible.

How lovely when God covers up our flaws and blemishes—especially as pastors' wives. We know we're very, very flawed, but people just don't seem to notice. Instead, they shower us with encouragement. "I love you so much," they'll say. "You are such an inspiration to me." And you think, *Inspiration? If you could only see how rotten I really am.* But God doesn't allow them to see your imperfections. Isn't He wonderful? Oh, how I love the Lord! What would we do without Him?

So how do those flaws get there in the first place? Well, like the blemishes that appear on your face, some flaws are the result of improper cleansing. It's so important to keep yourself clean. Like David, who asked God in Psalm 139:24, "Point out anything in me that offends You" (*NLT*), we need to go daily to Him and say, "Lord, I need cleansing." Often, it's just a matter of negligence. We really want to be cleansed, but we don't take the time.

The beautiful thing about the Lord is when we ask Him to reveal our hearts to us, He doesn't only tell us about those flaws. He also tells us how lovely we are to Him, and how much we please and delight Him.

Now, just as we take special care of our eyes and our mouth when we're applying our makeup, we want to care for those things spiritually as well. Think about your eyes. What do you read? What do you watch on TV? What are you putting in front of your eyes on a daily basis?

Then there's the mouth. The experts now tell us we should use a pencil first to keep the lipstick from bleeding into those little lines—which some of you don't have, you sweet things. How blessed you are. They're coming, don't worry. But what about your spiritual mouth?

Psalm 34:13 tells us, "Keep your tongue from evil and your lips from speaking lies." I truly believe one proof that you have a proper fear of the Lord in your heart is refraining from speaking evil things and lies. But it's hard to do. The book of James tells us it's harder to tame a tongue

than it is to turn an enormous ship. The tongue is an instrument of wickedness, and only the Holy Spirit can tame it. So we need to spend time every day submitting ourselves to God and asking Him to cleanse us of all unrighteousness.

Never forget, daughter, that you are God's workmanship. You're His poem and you're precious to Him. He's doing a work in you now that you can't quite see. But one day, 1 Corinthians 13:12 tells us, we won't have to see in a mirror dimly, and we won't just know in part. We will see God face to face, and we will know what He knows now. We'll see the work He was doing in us while we were on the earth, and finally that work will have reached perfect maturity. Praise God that one day, "in the twinkling of an eye, the trumpet will sound, and the dead will be raised incorruptible, and we shall be changed" (1 Corinthians 15:52). We shall be changed! All the flaws and blemishes and imperfections will be gone, and our corruptible bodies will be perfected. And we will be in the likeness of Jesus Christ.

Chapter Seven

THE GIFT OF BROKENNESS

*W*HEN YOU'VE been in the ministry a few decades, you would think you've got it pretty well together come Sunday morning. Wouldn't you? I did too. But one Sunday morning during first service, Chuck looked down and noticed a hole in his tie. At first he thought it was a moth hole, but we don't have moths, as far as I know. Regardless of how it got there, Chuck was mortified because at the end of first service he would be standing at the door wearing this tie, shaking hands with a long line of people.

But the Lord is such a wonderful provider. It happened to be Father's Day, and a young lady in the church felt moved to bring a gift for Chuck. And wouldn't you know it, she brought him a handsome, new tie. God took care of it.

Still, when I found out that he had gone to church with a hole in his tie, I was horrified. I talked with Chuck about it on the way home. I was still talking about it when we got inside the house, went upstairs, and got ready to take our afternoon nap. Chuck laid down on the bed, but I was still walking around our room talking. I said, "Now look, Chuck, both of us need to wear glasses when we choose anything to wear. On a Sunday morning, you can't be choosing your tie in the dark without wearing your glasses." I was in full lecture-mode—really pushing it in. "If you will get your suit out the night before, or if you'll let me choose your suit, I'll have your tie all ready." And I just kept going on and on. I was determined he would never wear a tie like that again. And at the height of my lecture, I walked over to our dresser and started taking my earrings off ... and saw, to my horror, that I had worn two different earrings to church.

Chuck already knew. I think he'd been waiting for me to get to the mirror. Rolling over, he put his face in the pillow and just laughed. You know, every husband longs for that to happen. Oh, I tell you, it's fun being a pastor's wife.

Actually, it really is wonderful. I wouldn't trade places with anybody or choose any other walk in the whole wide world. It hasn't been an easy road, mind you. It's been very tough at times. I've had my share of heartaches and grief. But I praise God that He would ever account me worthy of the privilege of touching lives and influencing people toward Him. I do not take the responsibility lightly—and I pray you don't either.

Years ago before the Iron Curtain fell, we had the opportunity to visit our missionary outreach in Millstatt, Austria. I'd wanted to go for years, but something had always prevented it. Our missionaries there were reaching people far beyond the Iron Curtain—Yugoslavians, Romanians, Bulgarians and Hungarians. It was a marvelous work, and every time I heard about it, my desire to go there grew. So I'd been praying that God would somehow open the door for us. Finally, one day I just said, "Well, I've laid it at the foot of the cross, Lord. If I never get to go, that's up to You. But You've let me go to every place else that I've ever wanted to go, so if it would please Your heart, would You allow this too?"

Then one morning, Chuck said, "How would you like to go to Germany?"

I answered, "If I can go to Austria too."

He said, "I knew you'd say that." As it turned out, he'd been invited to speak at a pastors' conference in England and in Germany … and in Austria. So my heart's desire was fulfilled.

In Millstatt, I met a pastor's wife who had come to the conference from her home in Yugoslavia. Olga was a woman devoted to the ministry—and a woman who understood hardship. Because of the poor dental care in Yugoslavia, she had lost all of her teeth by the age of thirty-two. Her husband was the pastor of not just one church, but ten churches, and all of them small. Up until the year I met Olga, she and her husband had not owned a car, but walked everywhere they needed to go. Olga worked twelve hours a day in a dry cleaning plant, where the temperature was between 98 and 110 degrees. When she came home from work each night, there were always people at the house who had come for counseling. And since the Yugoslavian custom is to cook dinner for people who visit, Olga cooked every night for all their visitors. Along with her husband and their two children, this usually meant cooking for fifteen people, on average.

Now, I want you to think about that for a minute. How would you feel if you worked twelve hours a day, six days a week, and you came home every night to cook dinner for fifteen people? I can't imagine doing that even if I didn't work at all! We have nineteen grandchildren and over twenty great-grandchildren, but they're not here all the time. When a big group comes to visit us, we usually take them out to a restaurant, unless it's a holiday. Every once in a while, Grandpa will get in the kitchen and make a mess with the kids. But for the most part, we take them out. Cooking for fifteen people? Every night? How many of us would do that faithfully, night after night—and without complaining?

Now add this to the mix: Olga had no kitchen! All she had was a tiny little room with one small burner. She only had one pot to cook with, and just a few plates. She had a table, a basin, and a very small, inefficient refrigerator. The food on the bottom wouldn't stay cold enough, and the food on top froze so hard it took forever to thaw. Yet she used what she had and she did it day after day with a joyful attitude in the Lord.

I had actually heard about Olga before I met her. One of the couples in our church, Hans and Vivian, met Olga and her husband when they were visiting Yugoslavia. Just before they came home from their trip, Vivian called me and shared how blessed she and Hans had been by this couple's brokenness and willingness to serve for Jesus.

Then Vivian suggested, "We were wondering if the women in the Joyful Life Bible study would like to furnish a kitchen for Olga." I asked her how much she thought it would cost, and she said, "I think we can do it for about five hundred dollars."

I knew our women would want to do this, so I told Vivian to get what she needed, and by faith we sent the check. In the days before Hans and Vivian came home, they were able to completely furnish a kitchen for

Olga—for only five hundred dollars. They painted the room, bought her some pots and pans, dish towels, hot pads, utensils, and most importantly, a little stove and a stainless steel sink. When Olga saw the sink, she exclaimed, "Oh, my! It even has the garbage place in the middle!" She was absolutely blessed.

So I already knew about Olga and her hardships before I got to Austria, and it affected me deeply. When we arrived at the pastors' conference on Friday night and walked in to the service, and I saw all the Hungarian and Yugoslavian people in front of us, I sat down and the tears started pouring down my face. In fact, most of our group had the same reaction. There were seventy-three people with us, and we all had been deeply moved by seeing these people from behind the Iron Curtain, knowing what a great price they paid to be in the ministry.

If you think life is hard, you should listen to some of the stories of life in Yugoslavia. The pastors and pastors' wives are viewed as the offscouring and scum of society. One pastor told us about a time he was brought in to the police department for possessing Maranatha Music tapes. "You have been spreading propaganda," they said.

"What have I done?"

Holding up the tape they had confiscated from his house, they said, "You are giving the people this music."

He said, "It's just the Bible—that's all. Listen to it."

They refused. So he asked again, "Please, listen to it."

Finally they began playing it—and kept playing it. Finally, in the middle of the first song the pastor asked, "Would you like a tape?"

"Ya, ya," they said. So now the police have a Maranatha Music tape. God is working in Yugoslavia.

How easy it is for pastors' wives in the United States to get spoiled! We don't have nearly the hardships that pastors' wives endure elsewhere in the world. Sure, we have our own difficulties, but really they don't compare. Sometimes the wounds we receive in the ministry can hurt us greatly. When our people treat us harshly and unkindly, it can lead to bitterness. I've known pastors' wives who become so bitter that they refuse to fellowship or even talk with their people anymore.

I doubt there's a pastor's wife anywhere who hasn't been wounded at some time in her life. Most of us have been battered, scarred and pushed around a little bit. In a world controlled by Satan, that's just the way it goes. But you can't allow those wounds to fester into bitterness.

I once knew a pastor's wife who, after she and her husband had left the church, sent back a letter to the people. I read it. It was an angry letter, full of accusations and blame, and it just dripped with her bitterness. I sat and cried when I read it. I thought, *Those poor people. Even if there were problems, she was a representative of the Lord Jesus Christ to them. She never should have spewed such ugliness to them.* Is that the way we want to represent Jesus? Never. We want to live in such a way that rivers of love flow from us to others.

Too often, we fail to realize that the hard things in life have been allowed by God. He has a reason for it. He has permitted it, but He has not permitted you to become bitter over it.

Not long after we returned from our trip to Austria, I woke up very early one morning and I immediately thought of something crushing that had happened there, something that had become my thorn. All I could do was to weep before the Lord. I prayed, "God, please take it away. I can't bear it any longer. But Lord, if You want it to remain, will You show me the purpose in it?" I felt the Spirit of the Lord say to me, "Kay, there isn't much in your life right now to break you or to keep you in brokenness. This thorn keeps you in a place of brokenness so that you're useful to Me. Are you willing to have this thorn keep you in the place of brokenness? My grace is sufficient for you." I bowed my heart and said yes, because God forbid that the thorn would be taken away and haughtiness or pride would come into my life and keep me from being useful to Him.

Brokenness is necessary to the Christian life. It sounds scary and unpleasant but if we're to be useful to God, it's essential. We want to be useful to Him, don't we? So we need to understand brokenness and we need to accept it. The simplest definition I can give you is this: Brokenness is living in the bright light of truth about myself as I am before God.

Do you remember what you were like when you first came to Jesus? I do. I was twenty years old, and although I had accepted the Lord when I was a tiny girl, I hadn't been living close to Him. In fact, I was very, very far from Him and I had even stopped believing in Him. That summer I had agreed to go to camp, and as I was sitting on this rock, listening to all these Christians around me singing and praising God—I suddenly knew there was a God. He was there, and I was broken and crushed before Him. I saw my sins in the holiness of His light, and I wept. I was sorry for those sins … and I knew I needed a Savior. I was broken. Brokenness did its work: it brought me to the feet of Jesus.

On that trip to Austria years ago, we had a meeting one afternoon where the women of the East met the women of the West. I found out

later that the Yugoslavian women had been terrified to meet us Western women, because the only thing they knew about Western women was what they had seen on TV. Apparently they had viewed television shows like "Dallas" and I guess they expected a lot of big hair and glamour. I don't know whether we disappointed them or cheered them up. But I do know that they had never seen such love poured out on them before, because they told us so. Jesus did what politics could never do. Jesus brought East and West together and we hugged. Yugoslavians don't really hug. They kiss on one cheek and then the other. But we just threw our arms around them and wrapped them in love, and they responded. It was a precious, precious moment.

Among the Yugoslavian women was one very beautiful girl about twenty years old by the name of Melinda. At the end of our meeting, one of the Yugoslavian pastors' wives prayed, and then I prayed. As soon as I finished, Melinda ran out of the room. Chuck was standing right outside and she ran by him and then stopped. He asked, "Are you all right?" Tears were streaming down her face, and he put his hand on her shoulder and said, "The Spirit of the Lord is upon you." She tried to say something to him but couldn't, so she turned and ran away.

We didn't see her again until later that evening. When we got back to Millstatt, our friend came to us and said, "Melinda needs help and she needs prayer. Will you come right away?" He took us to the basement of the building where Melinda was waiting. We began talking to her and she explained what had happened that afternoon. "When that pastor's wife prayed, something happened to me. I felt something come all over me and for the first time in my life, I was sorry for my sins." Tears gushed down her face. "I have never been sorry for my sins—never." She had been raised under communism, and unless your sin is a sin against the state, you're not expected to be sorry.

I saw her brokenness—and it was beautiful. Brokenness is our starting point with God. But it continues from there. Do we need a Savior any less today than we did the day we found Jesus? Do we need to be any less broken before Him? Do we need to have any less sorrow for our sins than we did then? No. We will never be anything more than sinners saved by grace. We will always need a Savior. You and I will always need to be as broken as we were the day we first confessed our sins.

When you're walking in the light of God's holiness, you acknowledge the sin in your life and you repent of it. Repentance is not just being sorry for your sin; it encompasses a change of mind and behavior. Too often we look repentant on the outside, but inside we're filled with anger toward our husbands, children, or the people in our church or the ministry. We're angry at life itself. But it's not enough to be nice on the outside. You need to deal with the darkness inside, or you will lose your fellowship with God.

> If we say that we have fellowship with Him, and walk in darkness,
> we lie and do not practice the truth (1 John 1:6).

When our fellowship with God is hindered, so is our fellowship with others. Some people think they can have everything right with God, but not with others. Not true. There is a vertical relationship and there's a horizontal relationship. I was speaking with a lady who was filled with wrath towards someone, and I said, "Oh, you've got to take that to the cross. You can't keep that to yourself."

She answered, "I have talked to the Lord about it. It's straightened out between God and me and that's all I care about." But she was wrong. She needed to be broken.

If we are not broken, our fellowship with our husband will not be right. Our fellowship with our children will not be right. Our deep, intimate, heart-to-heart communion with God and with others is completely dependent upon our brokenness.

I had the sweetest earthly father possible. Daddy and I were very close. He was the one I went to when I needed a heart-to-heart talk. But sometimes, when I was being a sassy little monster, Daddy would say, "Honey, I'm not going to talk to you again until you can talk to me with love." My misbehavior broke our fellowship—and that broke my heart. You know, my mother could yell at me and spank me, she could carry on—and all it did was toughen me. But when my daddy broke fellowship with me, I could not bear it. And I feel that way about my heavenly Father.

Some people think that being out of fellowship with God is not very important. But just think how you are affected when you are out of fellowship with your husband. I can't stand it. Chuck and I have learned to walk in brokenness with each other, and it has made all the difference in our marriage. Whenever we have to be apart—whether he's flying off to another country or we're just leaving each other for the day—we like to leave little notes for each other. He calls me "Kazy" and I call him "Captain Zoom-Zoom," because he's always zooming everywhere. Isn't that the most romantic name you've ever heard? But he's my dear Captain Zoom-Zoom.

Now, we didn't always have the sweet *koinonia* fellowship we do now—that desire to cuddle each other and leave love notes. So take hope if that's not where you and your husband are yet. But know this: it didn't come through criticism or through carping or through making demands. It came through brokenness. If you want the deepest, most intimate, loving fellowship possible with your husband, then you must be broken. You'll never get there by telling him what a rotten sermon he preached, or that he is a careless and negligent husband. It comes through the brokenness that reaches out and says, "Honey, I care about you. I love you." Remember that.

When our fellowship with God is broken, we are always the one at fault through our sin. God does not ever break fellowship with us—it is entirely our doing. Sadly, sometimes other people break fellowship with us, and they have no desire to reconcile. You can't control that. But don't ever let a broken fellowship be your doing. Always pray for reconciliation, and send sweetness whenever you have an opportunity to do so.

When we harden ourselves in our sin, and we resist brokenness, we lose fellowship and we lose our joy. That's what happened to David when he sinned with Bathsheba. He lost his joy. That's why he eventually came to the place where he begged God, "Restore to me the joy of Your salvation" (Psalm 51:12). Sin steals our joy.

Sin also extinguishes the light for our path. You can tell when someone is walking in darkness, can't you? They just start walking a little bit crazy. Have you developed a sensitivity where you can see that in others? Ask God to give you that discernment. You'll know something's wrong, because your fellowship is suddenly compromised. You used to be able to sit with that person and talk about the Word together, and they always had some wisdom from the Lord to share. And then it's gone. The things they say no longer line up with Scripture. Sin has blinded them to the truth.

Sin also blocks the fruit of the Spirit from working through our lives. That's because sin is really "self" being in control, and you cannot have it both ways. Either you control your life or the Holy Spirit controls your life. If you want the fruit of the Spirit to flow through you and out to others, then "self" needs to get out of the way.

One summer years ago, a big group of us went up to Bass Lake and stayed in a home some friends had loaned to us. It was a beautiful home right on the lake, but of course, everything in the house belonged to our friends—including the many antiques displayed everywhere. Now, we had quite a few of our grandchildren with us. And I remember that I couldn't rest. I was so tense and so afraid the children were going to break the antiques that I became obnoxious—truly obnoxious. Everything was "Don't." "Don't run! Don't touch! Don't roughhouse!"

My family kept looking at me with that "Oh, Mom" look. You know the one. Several times I went upstairs to our bedroom and pleaded with the Lord to help me to relax. But then I'd go back downstairs and see one of the kids running and I'd start in again. Finally, after a few days, I couldn't stand myself anymore. I walked back upstairs and started praying, "God, You have given me Your Holy Spirit— why isn't He working through my life? Why isn't love, joy, peace, and longsuffering flowing through my life? What is the matter with me?"

I really wanted Him to say, "Bless you, darling. You're just a grand-mother and it's perfectly all right, you poor thing. I know you're high strung and tightly wired." But do you know what He spoke to my heart? He said, "There's sin in your life. There's anger, and impatience, and …" He was gentle as He went down the list, but He didn't miss a single one.

I stood there listening, and then I said, "Oh, Father, I am so sorry." And then I named the things back. I agreed with God about my sin.

How in the world could I have joy flowing through my life when I was angry at the imperfect people around me?

After I repented of those things, the channel was opened and I could feel the sweetness of the Holy Spirit flowing through me. Now, this is not to say that the tension didn't creep up again. It would, and I'd have to confess it again to the Lord. I had nothing to blame it on but my sin. I couldn't even blame it on PMS anymore. I suppose I could have tried blaming it on the change of life. But it wasn't that. It was sin, and there's no pill for sin. Estrogen doesn't work on sin, does it?

The only thing that works on sin is confession and repentance. When God says there is sin in your life, you say, "Yes, Lord, I agree with You. I confess it before You." Call it by name as He reveals it. If He hasn't named it for you, say, "Lord, please show me exactly what that sin is." First John 1:9 promises, "If we confess our sins, He is faithful and just to forgive us our sins and to cleanse us from all unrighteousness."

How beautiful that God has made a way for us to walk continually in the light of His fellowship. Darkness hides sin, but God's light reveals it. We can't be afraid of His light. We don't want to be Christians who walk around with one little dim flashlight. "Okay, Lord," they say. "Show me one sin. But don't show me any more. I'll take care of this one but I don't want to see the rest of them."

Sin loves darkness, and it loves secrecy. People who are in sin are quick to put on a mask to hide who they really are. And in so doing, they keep other people at bay. Usually we have an awareness when someone is trying hard to pretend to be something they aren't. You just know you're not getting to the real person inside. You can never get close to someone who is wearing a mask—it's not even possible. But when you're around a genuine, transparent, broken person—a person who

is not afraid of the light of God's holiness but actually welcomes it—you're completely drawn to them. You have instant fellowship with them. They're not trying to be super saints and they're not worried about trying to impress you—they're just real. They're natural. Chuck is that kind of a Christian. Whether he has a hole in his necktie or not, he's just Chuck.

Aside from the masks and the secrecy, the one who resists brokenness is irritable, prideful, envious, critical, resentful, jealous and anxious. They are self-focused and self-centered, and will fight with anyone who tries to take away their rights. They indulge in a lot of self-justification, and care very little about making things right with others. They are self-promoting—always seeking their own glory rather than God's.

That's a horrible list, isn't it? We need to pray and ask God to root out any of those sins that may be present in our hearts. But as a pastor's wife, pray especially against that last one. May it never be said of you that you stole glory from God. If someone else comes into the church and she sings better than you or she speaks better, let her be used in your church. I played the piano often in our ministry, but I always told Chuck, "When somebody comes in who is better than I am, please let them play." From time to time that would happen, and I was always happy to move over and let them play. Then, when they'd move away, I'd have to step back in. I loved playing the piano. But I didn't love it to the point of insisting. It didn't matter who played—it only mattered that God was glorified.

Now, I'm not one to like formulas as a rule, but sometimes things do follow a formula. And in the measurement of our brokenness, this happens to be the case. The measure of your brokenness—which is also a measure of your spiritual maturity—is equal to the time it takes for you to make things right. It's equal to the time it takes for you to become aware of your sin, confess it, repent of it, and ask for cleansing.

For example, let's say you're sitting in your chair on a Sunday morning listening to your husband, and all of a sudden, he decides to use you as a bad example in the sermon. Thankfully, Chuck has never done this to me, but I know it happens sometimes. Maybe you came to church just full of joy that morning, but now you're horrified. All you can think is, *This whole congregation is going to think I'm a horrible person—and I don't have equal time to get him back!* Your pride rises up and you decide you're going to really straighten him out the minute you get the chance.

So that's exactly what you do. The moment you get alone in the car, you start in on him. "How could you do that to me? How could you let all those people think badly of me?" It's understandable. We don't want to be thought of badly. The "self" wants to be admired, pampered, cherished, and thought of as beautiful, wonderful and marvelous. So you let him know with a big, wordy lecture just how wrong he was.

Or maybe you don't say a word at all. Maybe you give him the silent treatment for a few days, just to make him suffer. Women like to pout, you know. But eventually, you speak again and you let him know just how much he's wronged you.

Remember, the measure of your brokenness is equal to the time it takes for you to make things right. Some women need days and days before they see their pride for what it is, confess it to the Lord, and repent and become cleansed. Others need twenty-four hours. Others need only half an hour … or a minute … before they realize that as hard as it is to be used in the sermon as a bad example in front of the congregation, if it helps to get the point across, then to God be the glory. It's only

when we highly esteem ourselves that we're bothered with this sort of thing. But when we're willing to be known as servants of the Lord Jesus Christ, when we're broken and we're willing to be broken further, we're not going to care about it. We're not going to stand up for our own rights.

The one who is spiritually mature might start out with a lecture. She might. She might say to her husband, "I really wish you hadn't used me as an illustration this morning. I don't like it when you do that …" But the Spirit of the Lord interrupts her and says, "That doesn't please My heart. You're not walking in brokenness." And she quickly turns to her husband and says, "Honey, I shouldn't have said that. I'm sorry." Brokenness is being willing to say, "I was wrong."

I have a friend who got very angry at something someone in her family had said, so she went up to her room and stewed and fretted about it. She told me that at some point she looked down at her watch and realized she'd been angry for half an hour. She said to herself, "I'm just not broken." And she immediately went back and made it right with that person. That's a woman who is walking in brokenness.

So what are the marks of brokenness? The first thing is when you realize you've sinned, you have an immediate desire to make it right. Instead of holding on to that sin, you want to deal with it right then and there. Like my friend, let very little time pass before you repent of that sin and let God cleanse you.

Secondly, there's a lack of defensiveness. Even in those times when you've been misjudged, don't try to defend yourself—you leave it to God. Now, this is hard. I told you it costs. You let God take care of your reputation. He will do it. If you walk in brokenness, God will defend you.

I don't think it's possible to be a pastor's wife and not have somebody someplace misjudge you, even if you're practically perfect. Even the sweetest, dearest, most loving and least offensive pastors' wives are misjudged. It's going to happen. When it happens to you, just walk in brokenness. Let God take care of your reputation.

The third mark of brokenness is that you don't make excuses for your sin. God doesn't cleanse excuses—He cleanses sin. So when you're convicted of your sin, name it before Him. "Lord, I was critical." "I was dishonest." "I was bitter." The broken person wants to be clean before the Lord, so they have no interest in trying to justify their sinful behavior.

I think 1 Corinthians 13:4-7 is the best standard we can have for our lives.

> Love suffers long and is kind; love does not envy; love does not parade itself, is not puffed up; does not behave rudely, does not seek its own, is not provoked, thinks no evil; does not rejoice in iniquity, but rejoices in the truth; bears all things, believes all things, hopes all things, endures all things.

Now, none of us can maintain that standard every day. We're going to fail. As long as we are living in these bodies, we're going to sin. But we can walk in the light which brings the conviction of sin. Read 1 Corinthians 13:4-7 and check your life against it. If something needs to go, ask God to forgive you and cleanse you. Read it often. In fact, I believe every pastor's wife should know these verses by memory.

Brokenness is God's goal for us. Romans 8:29 tells us that we were predestined to be conformed to the image of Christ. That's what brokenness brings into our lives—Christlikeness. In order to bring us to that place of brokenness, God will use any number of methods.

One very effective method of breaking is trials. James writes, "My brethren, count it all joy when you fall into various trials" (James 1:2). The word "fall" in that verse has the same connotation as when a man journeying from Jerusalem to Jericho might fall among thieves (Luke 10:30). It's not something that comes upon you because you did something wrong—it just comes upon you. That's because God has a divine purpose in it. If you "count it all joy," and if you learn the lessons the Lord wants you to learn through the trial, you will be broken in certain areas and you will grow. I have never gone through a trial yet in which I haven't learned something about God and about myself.

I remember one Saturday morning when a man called the church and threatened to kill Chuck. I wasn't broken at all by that trial—not at first. Instead, I was filled with rage, anger and fear. You might think, *Well, I don't blame you.* But that's not what God said to me. Apparently, He did not want me running around the church asking, "Where is Chuck? Where is he?" and fearfully watching every car that pulled into the parking lot. He wanted me to remember that Chuck is in His hands. He wanted me to remember that I didn't have to walk in anxiety and fear. God wanted me to trust Him. So finally, I prayed, "God, You know how much I love Chuck. You know how much I need him, and You know how much Calvary Chapel needs him. But he's in Your hands, and I know You can restrain the hand of this man who wants to bring evil against him. So I entrust my precious Chuck to You." And then I went and cleaned my house.

That's what God wants. He wants to break us of our distrust and our anger and wrong reactions. But we so often look for a way out of the trial precisely because we don't want to be broken. We sometimes look around and think, *How did I get into this mess? What am I doing here? Where's the doorway out?* But the Lord says right back to us, "You stay there until you learn the lesson." How important it is to stay in that trial until it has done its work in us. Our attitude in our trials will result in either brokenness or bitterness.

Trials are one method God uses to break us. Another is failure. I had an embarrassing failure once that I would just as soon keep to myself, except that it's such a perfect example of how God will use those things to break us.

I was at a luncheon with friends from church and the subject of low blood sugar came up. As it happened, I was feeling really weak that day. Twice before while feeling like that I had blacked out, and I had diagnosed myself as having low blood sugar. I hadn't seen a doctor about it, but I was sure that's what I had.

My friends started talking about that very thing. One woman said to the other, "Joan, how's your blood sugar? How are you doing?"

Joan said, "Oh, I am so tired all the time."

I said, "Me too."

The next lady said, "Yes, I had low blood sugar and the doctor gave me some good advice for that."

The lady next to her said she had low blood sugar ... and then the fourth woman said she did too. So I piped up. "I have it too."

One of the women asked, "Oh, did you go to the doctor?" Now, it would have been so easy to say, "No, I haven't been yet." But that's not what I said. Instead I said, "Yes." My reputation was at stake, you see. I wanted to be as bad off as they were.

At the end of lunch, we all said goodbye and I got into the car to start driving home. And I started talking—partly to myself, and partly to the Lord. "Oh, what did I do? Why did I say that? Lord, what am I going to do now?"

Chuck got home right after I did, and he walked in to the sight of tears pouring down my face. "Honey," he said, "what happened at the luncheon? Didn't you have a good time?"

I said, "I lied. I lied!"

"What did you lie about?" he asked.

"I told them I had low blood sugar."

He said, "Well, I thought you did have low blood sugar."

"I know you thought I did, and I thought I did too, but I told them I had gone to the doctor about it."

"You mean you've not gone to the doctor?" he replied.

"No—I lied. That was my lie!"

Chuck was shocked. After a minute, he commented, "You know how you have to make it right."

I nodded, "I know." In order to make it right, I had to call every one of those women. Chuck didn't tell me I had to do it. He let me choose. But the Lord required it of me. And my friends? They laughed their heads off. They thought it was the funniest thing. But it wasn't funny to the Lord and it wasn't funny to me. And I'll tell you, that was the best tongue-tamer ever. Boy, whenever that thought pops into my mind now and I get the urge to say "Me too" about something, I remember the lesson I learned through my failure.

Our failures can work beautifully to break us. I think about when we moved to Costa Mesa, way back in the beginning of our ministry at Calvary Chapel. Chuck looked very strong and stalwart on the outside, but he was a broken man on the inside. He'd already spent seventeen years in the ministry and he had given it his all. He had preached his best sermons and he had been as winsome and darling as could be. And after seventeen years, we were moving to a church of twenty-five people. He was a broken man. But God's plan for Calvary Chapel could never have come into being by any other means than by a broken man, a broken pastor. God wants us to walk in brokenness.

Then there's chastening. God breaks us through chastening. Oh, how I hate chastening. But it's so necessary. Remember what David did after he sinned with Bathsheba? He came up with a plot to have her husband, Uriah, murdered. And it worked. David got away with both adultery and murder. God says in Psalm 50:21, "These things you have done, and I kept silent; you thought that I was altogether like you." In other words, "Because I don't send lightning down upon you when you sin, you think I don't see." The Bible tells us, "For the ways of man are before the eyes of the LORD, and He ponders all his paths" (Proverbs 5:21). God sees everything we do. He's watching.

Now, He's not watching us to catch us in our sin. He's watching us because He loves us and He wants to bring us to a good end. Therefore, one of His ways to deal with unbroken sons and daughters is through chastening. David's chastening came through the loss of his baby. It broke him and led him to write Psalm 51. You can hardly read it

without tears coming to your eyes. "Oh, cleanse me, Lord. I am so sorry. Against You and You only have I sinned. I've done this awful thing in Your sight. Oh, create in me a clean heart." That's the cry of a brokenhearted man who has been severely chastened by God.

So many wonderful things come through brokenness, such as spiritual revival. The awareness of our sin, and the brokenness which comes through that, renews our spiritual passion for the Lord. It causes our heart to long after God like the deer pants for the water. Can you say that today? Can you say, like the psalmist, "As the deer pants for streams of water, so my soul pants for You, O God" (Psalm 42:1 *NIV*)? Thirst is a great indicator of spiritual passion. When my thirst starts to slack off, I know there's something wrong in my life. Matthew 5:6 tells us, "Blessed are those who hunger and thirst for righteousness." If you want great blessings in your life, you must hunger and thirst after righteousness. Brokenness will naturally bring forth a thirst for God. You instinctively want to draw closer and to know Him better.

Everything in our flesh rebels against the idea of brokenness. But our spirit longs to be revived and renewed and refined—and this only comes through brokenness. Learn to see it as a gift. When trials come, accept them as coming from His hand. When chastening comes, see it as the loving correction of your Father. Let those tools do their work. Brokenness will make you a vessel of honor, fit for His use.

> In a great house there are not only vessels of gold and silver, but also of wood and clay, some for honor and some for dishonor. Therefore if anyone cleanses himself from the latter, he will be a vessel for honor, sanctified and useful for the Master, prepared for every good work (2 Timothy 2:20-21).

As the pastor's wife, you will never fulfill the ministry that God calls you to do unless you are broken.

The alabaster box that Mary brought to Jesus was beautiful. But the box itself couldn't minister. It didn't matter how smooth the box was to the touch or the quality of the alabaster itself. All that really mattered was the content of the box—the wonderful fragrance it held. As long as the box remained intact, the content was hidden away. It blessed no one. But broken? Once the box had been broken, it anointed Jesus Christ with love and the house was filled with its fragrance.

Crushing never feels good. But oh, beloved sisters, how precious it is when the fragrance of Jesus pours forth from you and blesses your husband, his ministry, and all the people God has put into your care. Be willing to be broken.

Chapter Eight

CONTINUALLY GUIDED

THERE WAS a time in our early ministry years when I thought I had all the answers. I just loved solving problems for people, and I couldn't wait for somebody needy to come along so I could fix them. But that was back when I was twenty-two—and I knew a lot more than I do now!

One Friday, as I was leaving the church after our Joyful Life Bible study, a woman stopped me at my car to say she needed some advice. She began describing her problem, which was really awful and quite serious. When she finished, she asked, "What do you think I should do?"

I didn't have the foggiest notion. So I said to her, "I'll pray with you, but I really don't know what you should do." Now, it took me a long time as a pastor's wife to gain the confidence to say, "I don't know." The fact is, we don't always know. Others might expect us to have all the answers, and we may have that same expectation of ourselves, but we simply don't always have the answer.

Thankfully, we have the promise of Isaiah 58:11:

> The LORD will guide you continually, and satisfy your soul in drought, and strengthen your bones; you shall be like a watered garden, and like a spring of water, whose waters do not fail.

What a comfort this verse is to me! God has proven it true time and time again. So when this woman approached me for advice, I was able to say with confidence, "I know if I am to be involved in any way, the Lord will guide me."

Aside from the pastor himself, I don't know of anyone who needs God's continual guidance more than the pastor's wife. Often she receives phone calls, one upon the other. She has to make quick decisions and offer prayers instantly. So if we desire God's strengthening and wisdom, and if we want to represent Him accurately to the people, then we need to wait on Him for guidance.

God opened my eyes to the truth of Isaiah 58:11 in a tremendous way several years ago. A couple with two little children had recently moved into our neighborhood. The wife was just darling. We chatted over the back fence a few times, and I discovered she used to go to a Calvary Chapel. Once, she even brought me a beautiful bouquet of flowers. Although we didn't have a lot of contact, we felt comfortable with each other. Then one night she called me in tears. "Kay, I think I'm losing my mind—I just threw the whole dinner on the kitchen floor." She then said, "I don't know what I'm going to do … my husband has left me. Can you come over?"

We hung up and I sat for a minute before the Lord. While I did so, the promise came back to me: "The Lord will guide you continually." Then I did something I had never done before.

Chuck was in his office studying on the computer. I walked in and said, "Chuck, our neighbor just called and she wants me to come over. Will you go with me?"

He was deep into his study. "No, no," he said, "you go."

I asked a second time. "Oh please, go with me."

Again, he said no. "Honey, you're used to doing this. You go."

I had never asked Chuck to go on a visit with me before. I'd always felt fine going alone. But this time was different—I just believed he was supposed to go with me. So I pleaded a third time, "Please go with me."

Still looking at his computer, he said, "No, you go on without me." I thought, *Lord, You promised to guide me. Please show me what to do.*

I felt quite strongly that I was not to go alone. So I turned around and I said, "Okay, if you're not going, I'm not going either."

Chuck had never heard me say anything like that. He looked at me, thought a moment, and said, "Okay, then. I'll go with you."

I was so relieved. I really wanted to go, because I knew the Lord wanted to use us to minister to our neighbor. Together we walked to her house, and when she opened the door she fell into my arms sobbing.

"What can I do?" I asked, hugging her back.

Between sobs she said, "The food's all over the kitchen floor …"

Chuck had already seated himself, so I told her to sit and talk with him while I cleaned up the kitchen and occupied their adorable little three-year-old son.

In less than twenty minutes I saw the guidance of the Lord, because suddenly the front door opened and her husband came back unexpectedly. I knew then why the Lord had impressed on me that Chuck needed to be there. He walked in and sat on the couch next to his wife. Chuck started talking to them both and I could hear their conversation from the kitchen. Chuck shared with them the most beautiful words about marriage and why marriage is ordained of the Lord. He spoke with them for over an hour. At one point I peeked in and saw the husband sitting on the edge of the couch, taking in every word. And right before they ended their conversation, Chuck was able to pray with them. By the time the three of them came into the kitchen, the husband and wife had their arms around each other. It was glorious.

The next day my neighbor called me again. "Kay, you'll never believe what happened!" She shared that after Chuck and I had left, her husband took her upstairs, knelt by the side of their bed, and asked God to forgive him for everything he had done to make such a wreck of their marriage. He then asked God to make him the man that He wanted him to be. "Then," she said, "he took me into his arms and told me how much he loved me and that he was sorry for all the years he had treated me badly."

The Lord wants to guide you continually—and He will, if you'll just wait on Him and let Him speak to you. Don't we all want that guidance? Oh, we need it! Things often happen unexpectedly and it seems we are usually the ones asked to fix them. Without the Lord, we won't have any idea what to do.

We once had a lady in our church who was a bit strange. For whatever reason, she felt compelled to wander through the back rooms of the church, and even into our office, opening closets and drawers and looking into files, pulling out anything which seemed interesting to her. Numerous times we would walk into a room and find her going through papers and making a mess of things. The elders had told her to stop rifling through the files—not just once, but several times. She kept on doing it. Again and again she was asked to stop.

Then one day as I was coming back from lunch, this woman—who had always been very sweet to me—met me in the parking lot with tears streaming down her cheeks. My immediate thought was, *Oh, I'm too tired for this one.* Have you ever felt that way? We get so tired in our own strength that we don't have anything of value to give to others. But, "the Lord will guide you continually."

Before I could ask her what was going on, she said, "Well, I'm not coming back to this church anymore."

"Why not?" I asked.

"Because they just kicked me out."

Now, I knew that couldn't be true. They hadn't done it yet and I didn't believe they had done it this time. So I told her, "Oh, they wouldn't do that."

"Yes, they did," she insisted. "And now I'll never see you again."

Then I felt the Lord's guidance.

"Come with me," I said.

Still crying, the woman followed me back to the office. I had her wait in a chair and then I hurried into Chuck's office. "Did you kick her out?" I asked.

"No," he said. "I wouldn't do that. We just told her not to go behind the counters again."

I was then able to assure the woman of what Chuck had said. I told her, "You weren't kicked out. They've only asked that you not get into the files again."

She came back the next Sunday and went through the files once again— but at least she was in church. I didn't know what we were going to do with her. But I knew the Lord would guide us continually. He is faithful.

The Lord will continually guide you. When you don't know what to say or do in a situation, wait on Him. He will faithfully lead you and give you the strength and the words for the situation. But if we're to hear and understand the Lord's guidance, we must walk with Him. We must be cleansed. If we're walking on a path that we shouldn't, then we cannot expect to have the guidance we need.

Sometimes a woman will ask to speak with me, and she'll begin to describe her situation. It's clear to me that she's gotten herself entangled in something she should not be, but then she'll try to justify it using Scripture. She'll say, "I've prayed about this and God showed me a verse for my situation." We'll look at it together—and if you squint at it just right, and if you ignore every verse that speaks against the thing she's doing, you could maybe argue that it supports her behavior. Sort of. Except you know it doesn't, because God never contradicts His Word. I can see the truth of the matter because I'm not on the path she's on and

I'm not trying to justify this behavior. I've had to say, "I'm sorry, but that's not quite right. That doesn't add up."

Because this woman isn't walking clean before the Lord, she isn't receiving the clear guidance of the Lord. She's listening to the deceptions of the enemy and convinced that she's hearing from God. Let me say this again: If you want God's guidance, you must have daily cleansing. You must desire to be right with the Lord. You must submit yourself to His leading and ask Him to show you your attitudes and actions which are displeasing to Him.

There will never be a time when this is not necessary. Just because you get old doesn't mean your flesh behaves better. It doesn't. Your flesh will continue to stir you up as long as you are breathing. It will make you jealous or touchy or overly sensitive so that you take offense at little things.

Not long ago I was with a large group of people on a cruise. These were people we knew really well, and we were having a marvelous time fellowshipping together. Then this lovely lady whom I adored, walked into the room. She approached the crowd a little bit awkwardly and started greeting the people in front of us. Then she greeted Chuck and she greeted the people on my other side and continued to greet people all around me ... but she never said one word to me.

Now, I am used to that, to be honest with you. As Chuck's wife, I'm used to standing at his side and people barely noticing me. And because I am a bit shy, I've never minded it. I love being with Chuck and seeing people love and adore and appreciate him. It's a precious blessing for me. But for some reason, on this particular night, something was very wrong with me. In the flesh, I let myself get offended.

Once we were back in our room, I admitted to Chuck how I was feeling. I told him I knew it was wrong and I needed to repent. I didn't want to repent, to tell you the truth, except that I knew I was wrong. I knew this would create a wedge between God and me if I didn't repent, and it would hinder His guidance. So I asked Him to forgive me and to fill me with His love for this adorable lady. I also asked Him to help me be right about the situation and maybe grow up a little bit.

A few days later, I was in another room on the ship, and the woman came over to me and said, "I've wanted to talk to you this whole cruise." I didn't tell her about the offense—but I was so glad the Lord had guided me immediately into repentance. We had a lovely time talking and catching up—all because God had dealt quickly with my flesh.

Keep short accounts with God. Deal with your sin the moment you're aware of it. Run quickly to the cleansing He offers, because we don't want to lose a moment of His guidance. We need it so desperately! And our people need it to be flowing through our lives. As the wife of a pastor, your people look to you for answers. You don't have them, but if you stay close to the One who does, you will always have something to give them. Though some might argue with this, I do believe that pastors' wives should live closer to the Lord than almost anybody. Certainly we need to live as close to the Lord as the pastor himself. How else would we be able to minister comfort to the people? How else would we have godly discernment?

We need God's guidance, vision and discernment in all aspects of the ministry, as well as in our own homes. I do not know where I would be without it—especially in raising our boys. Our girls never gave me a difficult time, but the boys were another matter. I don't think I ever completely understood them. But God helped me. Sometimes the Lord gave me a word of knowledge about something and the boys would say, "Mom, how did you know that?" Then they'd tell their friends, "Watch out. My mom knows everything." I liked them thinking that. It wasn't always true, but it certainly was a big help.

Besides daily cleansing, if we want the clear guidance of the Lord, we also need to trust. Proverbs 3:5-6 tells us,

> Trust in the LORD with all your heart, and lean not on your own understanding; in all your ways acknowledge Him, and He shall direct your paths.

This doesn't just suggest that we consult God occasionally. We are to acknowledge Him in *all* our ways. It is a promise that if we do, God will direct our paths.

Part of acknowledging God is waiting upon Him. We live in a speedy, hurry-up world and we often approach God that way too. We'd like His guidance right now. Well, God does not operate on our timetable. If we want to hear from Him, we need to wait on Him.

Often, with my Bible on my lap, I'll just sit and meditate on one passage. There's so much in the Bible I don't understand yet, so I'll be still before the Lord and say, "Lord, I want to know You more." That's God's desire too, so He always blesses that request. He is pleased when we take the time to wait on Him.

It's a fact of life that when we really want to do something, we make time for it. God knows this. And He is blessed when we declare, by the use of our time, how much He matters to us.

I love to think of Psalm 23 as it relates to Isaiah 58:11. The One who promises to continually guide us is our Shepherd. And what is the work

of the shepherd? It is to guide the sheep. He tells us when to go and when to stop. As the wife of the pastor, all sorts of things are expected of us. But not everything is God's calling. We need to stay close to Him so we can hear "yes" and "no." We can trust God to be with us continually and to give us clear direction no matter what comes our way.

I have loved watching the young kids grow up in our church. It's such a joy to see little ones become teenagers and then grow into adults, especially as you watch their love for the Lord increase and mature. Some of them really stand out. I remember during the hippie days when Chuck would point out certain kids—Greg Laurie was one—and he'd say, "That one is going to be a pastor." I don't think he missed one of them. He just saw something special in them—a love for God that was going to lead them into the ministry.

One such boy was in the church office several years ago at the same time that I was. All of a sudden, we heard a horrible crash on the road in front of the church. We all went running out to see what had happened and found a girl about sixteen years old who had crashed her car between the church and our school building. Somehow she had hit the curb alongside the road, which caused her car to flip and roll over twice. By the time we got there, the car had come to a stop and she was hanging upside down, strapped in her seat.

We all rushed to the car, but then we stood there frozen for a moment. But this boy from our office walked right up to the window and asked, "Are you all right?" When he saw that she was pretty much in shock, he said, "Let me pray for you." He did so—and at the end of the prayer, she prayed with him saying, "In Jesus' name."

A week later, a long, handwritten letter arrived at the church. In it, the girl explained that her injuries had been confined to just a gash on her head and an abrasion on her shoulder. She didn't remember a lot about the accident itself, but she remembered very clearly what she felt when that boy was praying for her.

She wrote,

> "Never before have I felt the power of prayer so strongly. And never again will I doubt that the Lord is guiding me and carrying me through my life. There is no doubt in my mind the Lord has something planned for me."

Now, the week that this girl had her accident was the same week as the 9/11 attacks on New York and Washington, DC. In her letter, the girl shared that her brother was in Washington, DC at the time.

> "In general, this has been too much for one week, let alone for a lifetime. My brother is actually a mile from the Pentagon. So I know the Lord has been by his side too."

She continued,

> "I know I crashed in front of your church for a reason. Everything would be different if I hadn't because prayer was the difference. Someone up there was watching over me, and my entire life has taken on a new meaning. Many things just don't seem as important and I have really thought about who I am and what I want to fulfill with my life. You never realize how precious life is until it's almost taken away. I've realized how much greater a Christian I could be and how I've needed to rededicate my life to Him. Everything seems so meaningless and without purpose if it does not include Jesus Christ."

Little did that young man know when he walked toward that upside-down car, God was directing him to minister to this young girl. God was leading him. God had a divine purpose for everything which happened that day.

Likewise, when we trust the Lord and walk in daily fellowship with Him, we can be assured that He will give us the same faithful, continual guidance. You never know what divine purpose He is preparing for you today. Only He knows that—and only He can lead you straight to it.

Chapter Nine

FOR LOVE'S SAKE

*M*Y HUSBAND likes one kind of shoe. Just one. It's a very specific shoe, and if you've ever spent any time at all around Chuck, you know exactly what they look like, because that's the only kind of shoe he will ever wear.

He keeps two pairs of these shoes outside our bedroom closet. And usually, there are about six pairs—all identical—sitting in the garage just outside the door. I mean, they're absolutely identical. He buys the same exact shoes every time he needs another pair.

Now, the Kay Smith of sixty-two years ago would have had something to say about this little idiosyncrasy. She would have grilled Chuck. "Why just this one brand of shoe? Why six pairs? Why don't you try to branch

out a little?" But I don't say any of that. Instead, I've learned to look at those shoes and be grateful for the man in my house who wears them. It's tender to me. I know that may sound a little crazy, but I've learned to be grateful for that row of shoes. Sometimes some of them will be unlaced, and I don't know why, but it just causes all these tender feelings to well up in me. So I'll pray for Chuck just before I get in the car, and I'll thank God for giving me that man for a husband. Chuck likes those shoes. And because he likes them, I want to like them too. I want to do it for love's sake.

And you know what? Chuck does things for me too for love's sake. Does your husband like to make the bed? Chuck doesn't. Maybe it never crosses his mind when I'm home, because he knows I'll do it. But after I've been away on a retreat, I'll go upstairs to our bedroom and see that he's made the bed. It's so much nicer to walk into the room with a made-up bed rather than one all crumpled and messy. He knows I'll like that, so he does it for me—for love's sake.

I'll tell you another secret. Chuck has never had coffee in his entire life—not a drop. And I love coffee. So Chuck, who is usually the first one up, makes my coffee every single morning—even on Sunday. He's up by five on Sunday mornings, and I get to wake up to a fresh pot of coffee waiting for me. Isn't that precious? Is that love? It's love.

We need that kind of love flowing in our marriages. We need it flowing through our lives. When we have this *agape* love, we will look for ways to love and bless others. We'll think, *What can I do for my friend so she knows I love her? What can I do for that difficult person at church to show my love to her?* That *agape* love, which flows from God through us and out to others, never fails. We need the empowering of God to love others as we ought to and to do the ministry He has called us to do. However, without it, our actions will tear down rather than build up.

Ministry is full of difficult moments—moments that sap every bit of your energy and your patience. If you're a new pastor's wife, you may not have encountered very many of them yet. But if you've been in the ministry for a while, you are probably amazed at just how tough it can be at times. Most of us were not prepared for that. So how do you get through those moments, those situations when people have big needs and they're looking to you for answers?

If you've had little ones, think back to those middle-of-the-night feedings when you crawled out of bed. I can so clearly remember waking up at three o'clock in the morning because one of my babies was crying in the other room. You're tired when that happens, aren't you? Maybe you've only been in bed a little while because that same baby needed rocking just a few hours earlier. How you'd love to stay in your warm bed and continue sleeping! But you don't, do you? No. You get out of bed and you pick up your baby. Then you diaper him and hold him and feed him—all the while whispering comforting words to him. Why do you do that when your body is begging for sleep? You do it because love compels you. Nothing else on earth will motivate you like love. You do it for love's sake.

So you know how to operate for love's sake. You do. Now you just need to transfer that knowledge over to the ministry. The first thing you must do, if you're to love the people in your church with *agape* love, is to make sure it resides in your heart. If *agape* love is to be operative in your actions, it must first be present in your heart.

Love for Jesus is the beginning of love for others. But a lot of times, we want to settle for loving only Him. We sing that old favorite, "I love You, Lord," or another worship song that declares our love for Jesus, and we're so moved that we feel like we'd do anything He asks.

But then someone in the church acts obnoxiously toward us, and we decide we want to give up the ministry. "I don't like that person and I'm never going back to that church again. I don't want to be a pastor's wife anymore. I'm through." But our love for Jesus should compel us to love His sheep too—even the difficult ones.

In the Greek language, the word "*agape*" refers to the self-sacrificing love God poured out on mankind through the cross. It's Christ's love. It isn't a romantic notion or a sentimental ideal. It's the love that our Lord Jesus Christ demonstrated on the cross.

Do you ever contemplate the depth of love that took Jesus to the cross? There's never been a more selfless act—not ever. Jesus, who was utterly sinless, took our sin upon Himself and bore the penalty of those sins, all for love's sake. He allowed the soldiers to drive nails through His flesh and raise His tortured body up on that cross for love's sake. He endured the one and only separation He ever had from His Father—who could not look upon all the sin heaped upon Jesus—all for love's sake. He did all that because He loved us. Love compelled Him to put our needs ahead of His own.

That's what God is asking us to do as pastors' wives. And it runs contrary to every message our culture gives us. All day long we hear: "Me, me, me. Me first." You hear it everywhere. "If it pleases me, I do it. If it doesn't please me, I don't do it." This is why our society is a wreck. This is why so many marriages break up. I'm so very tired of hearing women say, "I just don't love him anymore." Sometimes you feel that way—but so what? You get past that minute, that hour, or that day. You ask God to renew your love for your husband. You persevere.

I absolutely adore the ground Chuck walks on. I really do. I have never been happier in my marriage than I am today. But we had our moments back when I was much younger. Every couple has to grow and change. We did too. Each couple has to learn to appreciate the differences between them—and they really are precious differences. And now we're reaping the blessings of our commitment to one another. I'm so grieved when I think of all the marriages that could have survived and thrived if one person or the other hadn't given up too soon.

If ever there was a time when our churches needed to see pastors and their wives loving one another, it is now. We need to be an example for people who do not know how to love one another as they should.

I remember on our trip to Austria many years ago when a great number of people from the Eastern Bloc countries came to the Lord. What we heard from these new converts was so telling. They said, "We've seen a lot of Americans, but when we watched the pastors and their wives, there was something different about them."

One girl told me, "I kept going back, not because of what they were saying, but because of what I saw. There was a love, a tenderness between them." The Russian women weren't used to seeing men treat their wives like that, giving honor to the women and treating them with respect. I heard the same thing from a man in Romania. He said, "I looked in the preacher's eyes and I saw something I'd never seen before." It opened his heart to listen and to receive the gospel.

You too are being watched. Just by virtue of your position, people are watching you. Women are scrutinizing you and searching for things in you they'd like to imitate. They want to be like you—or they *should* want to be like you. And they will, if you are being the influence that God has called you to be.

When we first came to Calvary Chapel, hardly anyone carried their Bible to church. They were just not in the habit of doing so. But it was my habit, and it was for two other women who had made the move to Calvary Chapel with us.

The three of us wanted to sit in the front row every Sunday. Besides, I played the piano, so it was helpful to sit up close. Chuck would say, "Turn to First John," and the three of us would open up our Bibles and turn to First John. I guess people noticed us in front reading along in our Bibles every week, because not long after, others started bringing their Bibles to church too.

Then the hippies came to church, accepted Jesus Christ, and started showing up with their Bibles tucked under their arms. All the old pictures and films show the hippie kids with their big old Bibles. I can't say for sure how much of an influence Lynn, Nancy and I had with that, but when we watched those precious hippie kids walking into church with their Bibles, we felt that God was showing us the fruit of our example. I love thinking back on that.

As women, we have not been given authority over the church as our husbands, but we have been given the opportunity to be an influence to others. And it's a tremendous influence. In prayer we can take authority, but in our behavior, we are to influence others with a sweet spirit—a gentle, caring, loving spirit. One of the blessings I have as a pastor's wife is when someone says, "Oh, Kay, I just wanted to tell you that you've been such an influence in my life." I may not even know the person. But somehow, Jesus touched and influenced her through me. It's never me. It's never you either. We can't do anything of eternal value, but Jesus can—if we're willing to be His representative and love the people for Him.

Don't you long to be used by God to influence others? I know you do. I'm so very tired of Christians—and particularly pastors' wives—who are not the influence they could be and ought to be. I don't mean you have to stand on the street corner with a big sign proclaiming Christ. I'm talking about being an influence in your everyday life—at the market, while picking up your children from school, wherever you go. Most importantly, I'm talking about being the influence you should be in your home and in your church. Oh, how God wants you to be a woman who walks in love!

Sometimes pastors' wives get the wrong idea about their role. Your job is not to waltz in on Sunday morning wearing some little dress and stand around waiting for everyone to tell you how cute you are. That's not what God has called you to do. He's asked you and me to represent His Son to the people. We are to be closer to Jesus than anyone else in the church. We're to be as close to Him as our husbands are. We're to love His Word. We're to love the ministry. And we're most definitely to love the people in our church. If you do those things, you will be the biggest blessing to your husband's ministry. If you don't, you will be the biggest hindrance.

When *agape* love is in action, it compels you to make the right choices. Instead of naturally being prone to make a selfish decision, you choose to do what is best for others. That's the power of *agape* love. I would like to share with you just a few examples of how your life—and your ministry—will change when you decide to speak and act for love's sake.

LOVE MAKES YOU THINK TWICE.

We have never made a lot of rules for the pastors and pastors' wives who are affiliated with Calvary Chapel Costa Mesa. But we hope that you will love your people enough to set a good example for them.

I'm talking specifically about dressing modestly. That's an issue for all Christians, not just pastors' wives, but it's especially important for you, because so many people are watching you and will imitate what you do.

I ran into a pastor's wife who was wearing a shirt with such a low, plunging neckline that I was absolutely horrified. People were looking at her and I thought, *How can she be a pastor's wife and dress like this?* We represent Christ wherever we go. Because of that, we need to watch our necklines and our hemlines. We shouldn't be wearing skimpy dresses. Of course, it's not an issue for an old fuddy-duddy like me, but if you're a young pastor's wife, think about the example you're setting when you wear immodest clothing.

You might think this is a silly thing not worth worrying about. But you're wrong about that. Do you know who in the church appreciates your modesty? The other wives do. They want their pastor's wife to be a representative of Christ—not a cute, sexy little thing who is always turning their husbands' heads. They don't come to church to feel threatened by you. They come to learn about Jesus and to draw closer to Him. I don't care if you're twenty-one or ninety-one—conduct yourself in a way that brings glory to God. Dress in such a way that if Jesus came right now to take you home, you wouldn't be ashamed of what you're wearing.

When you look at it in this light, love will compel you to dress carefully. You won't feel like your liberty in this area has been taken away when you do it for love's sake.

LOVE GETS US THROUGH THE THINGS WE DON'T WANT TO DO.

You know that feeling when someone asks you to do something, and your heart sinks? You think, *Please don't bother me with this. I really don't have time today. I have other things—better things—to do.* Usually, it's something that's just not as important to you as it is to the other person. We all have those moments. I had one when someone in the neighborhood came by and asked for a favor. My immediate thought was, *Oh, I don't want to do this at all.* But then the Lord spoke to me, "You need to do this for love's sake." So I did. It didn't take long at all. And afterwards I thought, *Oh Lord, thank You for prompting me to help. I'm glad I did this.* When we act for love's sake, there is always a blessing.

The secret to acting for love's sake is relinquishment. In Luke 9:23, Jesus taught us that the cost of following Him is a denial of self.

> If anyone desires to come after Me, let him deny himself, and take up his cross daily and follow Me.

To deny yourself is to relinquish everything. "I am completely Yours, Lord. I will do whatever You ask me to do."

I've noticed that it's easier to relinquish in some settings than in others. For instance, it's easy to relinquish when we're at a retreat, isn't it? Whatever needs doing, we're willing to do it. When someone else has a need, we're happy to minister to her. And we do it sincerely—from the very depths of our heart. But then we go home ... it's not so easy there. Some need presents itself to us and we have an attitude. The old behavior rises up again and we struggle to relinquish.

Once you learn to let love be your motivation, it becomes easier. You might still have an initial attitude. But then you'll feel a check from the Holy Spirit, and you'll remember. "Oh yes. For love's sake." The more you operate out of love and let that motivate all you do, the more you'll grow to be like Jesus, and the more you'll grow into the woman—and the pastor's wife—that He desires you to be.

Your flesh gets so alarmed when you begin to act out of love instead of out of your selfish impulses. That's because the flesh thinks the only way to find fulfillment is if the big "I" is in control. But the truth is, you'll never find fulfillment that way. When "self" is in control, you indulge yourself—and that is a teensy bit fulfilling—but it's short-lived. The only way to have true fulfillment in this life is to relinquish yourself to Jesus and let His *agape* love motivate all you do.

LOVE SEES OTHERS THROUGH GOD'S EYES.

It's just a matter of fact that from time to time, someone will come into your church whom you just don't care for much. You know you should, but you just don't feel that *agape* love for them. When that happens, you need to ask the Lord to fill you with His love for that person. Pray, "Lord, please love them through me. Let me not hold anything against them. Let me just love them."

Anytime I've asked the Lord to help me with this, He has done it. He's so faithful. He never fails. He wants us to love His people, so when we ask Him to fill our hearts with the love we need, He always does.

The precious ones, of course, are easy to love. And He always sends some precious women to pray for us and encourage us. They bring us little gifts that we don't deserve. So often they are the balm to our hearts that God knows we need.

Then there are the difficult ones. They are a gift to us too, only we don't usually look at them that way. God brings them for a different purpose. He allows them in our lives precisely so we will learn to deny ourselves. Without them, we'd quickly become spoiled brats, wouldn't we?

I think most pastors' wives have at least one person who needs us desperately. This one loves to call us—usually more often than we're comfortable with. They give us opportunities to deny ourselves on a regular basis. God reminds us to be patient, kind and loving with them. He says, "This one has a need."

One darling lady used to call me quite a bit. She was older and very precious. All she really wanted was for someone to listen to her, so I would do that. Some days it was very hard for me because I had so many things I needed to get done. Those were the days when I would nurture her and exercise patience simply for love's sake. Other times, I really enjoyed talking with her. Thankfully, she was always so good about getting off the phone when she knew I was expecting Chuck. I'd just say, "You know what? Chuck's due home any minute."

She'd always reply, "Oh, let me get off the phone right now." She was just very sweet about it. And it was good for me to learn to be patient and to see her as someone Jesus brought for me to love.

Love must be our motivation. If we don't let love motivate us, then self will. And that always leads to disastrous results.

Many years ago there was a woman who served in our women's ministry. Not only was she beautiful and dressed just perfectly, but in all her service she always went above and beyond what was required. But she didn't have a love for the women. She took offense at someone else in the ministry, became very obnoxious, and started doing some strange things … and she lost her ministry.

Not long after this woman left our church, she ran into someone I knew and complained to her. The woman grumbled, "They never did appreciate me. I did all those things to get promoted and I never was." I was shocked when I heard that. We never dreamed self-promotion was her motive for serving. She did everything so beautifully and perfectly.

We'd always thank her and tell her how blessed we were, thinking she had done it for Jesus and for us. But she had an ulterior motive, and in the end, it was revealed.

I think it's good to question yourself about these things and to check your motivation. I'd like you to look at the following questions and answer them honestly. If you find an answer you're not happy with, ask the Lord to change you. Ask Him to fill your heart with His love.

- When I don't want to do something, but know I should, do I have a sweet spirit or a sour spirit?

- How do I treat the difficult ones in our church?

- How do I react when someone in the church doesn't like me?

- How do I respond when someone in the church offends me?

- How do I behave when someone in the church talks against me?

These last three can be very tough … but it all goes with the territory, beloved. People are people, and sometimes they can be very cruel. And we're human too, so we can get our feelings hurt. However, we must never allow bitterness to creep into our hearts.

Instead, we need to bring those hurt feelings to the foot of the cross and seek help from the only One who can change the situation. "Lord, fill me with love for that person. Give me so much love that it spills out of me and onto her. Make it so that I can't even think of a retaliatory thing to do to her." This needs to be our habit.

As the pastor's wife, you're going to have many, many opportunities to go to the cross in this way. But that's a good thing. It's at the cross where we find the strength to love as we ought. Be thankful you're a pastor's wife. Deny yourself, take up your cross, and follow Jesus wherever He leads you. Serve your husband and your people for love's sake and your church will respond, "There's a woman who walks with Jesus."

Chapter Ten

FAITH THAT WITHSTANDS "ALTHOUGHS"

I HAD ALWAYS liked Habakkuk chapter 3, but it wasn't until I went through a personal tragedy—a time of great sadness and grieving—that this passage really became my own. Have you found that to be true in your life? You read a verse over and over again, hear great teachings about that verse, and agree with it. You even have a fondness for it, but it really doesn't become *your* verse until you've actually had to lean upon it. That's how I came to love this portion of Scripture, especially the three verses at the end of the chapter.

My personal tragedy was just that—personal. I wasn't having a nervous breakdown or anything, but I was in a place where my joy was gone and nothing felt stable in my life anymore. Then one day I found myself reading Habakkuk. I didn't know a lot about the background of the

book—not nearly what I do now. But as I read verse 17, I realized Habakkuk was prophesying that when the Chaldeans invaded Israel, there would be absolute famine in the land. But he was also reminding the people that despite the famine, God is still worthy of praise.

> Although the fig tree shall not blossom, neither shall fruit be in the vines, the labor of the olive shall fail, and the fields shall yield no meat; the flock shall be cut off from the fold, and there shall be no herd in the stalls: *yet I will rejoice in the LORD, I will joy in the God of my salvation.* The LORD God is my strength, and he will make my feet like hinds' feet, and he will make me to walk upon my high places (Habakkuk 3:17-19 *KJV, emphasis added*).

I couldn't help but meditate on that first word "although." It is a powerful word in this context. Habakkuk is saying that although many bad things will happen, God is still worthy of our praise.

What is the "although" in your life today? Maybe it's, "Although we have a tiny church and we don't have enough finances to pay my husband's salary …" I've been there. I remember what that was like. Or maybe it's, "Although I don't feel loved …" or "Although the congregation is difficult …" We all have those "althoughs" in our lives. They come for a while and then they get resolved and disappear. We enjoy those restful, wonderful periods … but before long a different "although" comes along.

Some years back, we went to Hawaii so Chuck could speak at a conference, and we worked it out so that we could have a few days of rest together. I remember how precious those few days were with Chuck. We bought some papaya and cottage cheese to bring up to our room, and mostly we stayed right there talking and resting together. At that time we were both really tired and it was a much-needed break.

Now, our grandson was getting married in the middle of that month. We had initially planned to get home the night before the wedding, but then Chuck arranged for us to return home a little earlier. I was so thrilled because I didn't have a dress for the wedding. I thought, *Oh, now I'll have time to find something new to wear. After all, I am the grandmother.* Yet who pays attention to the grandmother? Nevertheless, I wanted to look okay.

So we flew out on Tuesday night and I was so happy to be home. I love Hawaii, but it was time to come back. The next morning I got up with vim and vigor and started down our stairway. And on the top stair I tripped. My ankle turned under and I sort of landed on it. I couldn't move—I just screamed. Chuck rushed over, picked me up and helped me get back to the room, where I laid in bed all day with ice packs on my ankle every twenty minutes. Fortunately, it wasn't broken—just sprained. Still, it was very painful.

While I was lying on the stairs waiting for Chuck to come help me, I prayed, "Lord, I am really impressed by Your Spirit to live out Habakkuk 3:17-19. I also want to be obedient to Philippians 4:4, where Paul said, 'Rejoice in the Lord always, and again I say rejoice.'" I had really felt impressed to obey those two Scriptures at that moment. Then I thought, *Now, Lord, I will rejoice—but may I ask You a question: What purpose do You have in this?*

I firmly believe there is a purpose in everything that happens. As it turns out, because I was lying in bed all day instead of out shopping for a dress, I had a wonderful chance to read, and I received three very serious phone calls that I may have missed otherwise. Not only that, if my mind had been on wedding plans instead of on rejoicing and trusting God, I might have viewed those phone calls as inconvenient interruptions to my plans—although, as we know, interruptions are the most important ministry of our day sometimes.

Many people were praying for my ankle and by the next day, although it was still ugly and blue and painful, it was slightly better. By the night of the wedding, I didn't have one ounce of pain. Although it was still swollen, and I could barely get my shoe on, I was able to make it down the aisle and to my seat with the help of an escort. The whole way, I kept praying, *Lord, You are so marvelous and merciful in all Your ways— Your goodness overwhelms me.*

My dress wasn't even an issue. I was able to find something comfortable right in my own closet. It was perfectly fine because, after all, I wasn't the most important one there. And it's always nice to wear something comfortable to a wedding.

I'd like to add that my sprained ankle was not the only "although" I faced that month … in the few weeks that followed, one thing after another popped up. I came down with an odd, painful infection and needed to start a dose of antibiotics. As though that wasn't difficult enough, some old friends of ours turned against us and a lawsuit reared up. On and on and on, the "althoughs" kept coming. Despite those trials, I learned something with each one, and I continued to stand on those verses in Habakkuk and Philippians. My trust in God grew week after week. I actually started a list and wrote out each "although" as it came. "Although I have a sprained ankle …" "Although I have this infection …" "Although we are being sued …"

As a result of the infection, I returned to the doctor for a blood test. Three days later he called to explain just how bad it was. He began with the bad news and ended with the worst. It's never good news when your doctor starts out by saying, "Now, Kay, I'm not going to hold anything back from you."

When I hung up the phone I sighed, "Oh, boy." I really hadn't been expecting that news. But the Lord said, "Rejoice." So I rejoiced because I knew that God is in control and has a plan for everything in my life.

A month later I had another blood test and it came back perfect. The infection wasn't even there. At first, they had run the test three times to make sure they had the right outcome. The doctor was very sure. Yet God is sovereign.

You know, studies have shown that rejoicing releases chemicals which are good for your brain and for your entire body. Don't you just feel the opposite happening when you're angry and sour? You can almost feel the bad chemicals manufacturing themselves and attacking your brain. But God's Word tells us, "A merry heart does good, like medicine, but a broken spirit dries the bones" (Proverbs 17:22). A merry heart is a rejoicing heart. It looks like science has finally caught up to God's Word on this issue.

What causes me to rejoice the most is the simple knowledge that God is with me. He has promised He will never leave me nor forsake me. I know He's with me every step that I take through this life. And beloved, you must come to that place where you trust Him fully. God wants you to trust Him. Trust is such a simple little word, but so difficult for some people to do.

Many Christians vacillate when something difficult comes along their path. But that's when we need to trust Him the most. That's when God's on the verge of delivering us. And when you've gone through a number of calamities and have seen firsthand how God walked you through each one, your faith is strengthened. You're quicker each time to turn to Him and place all your trust in Him.

I love the story Hannah Hurnard shared in *Hinds' Feet on High Places* [10] about Much-Afraid and her little bag of twelve pebbles, each of which represented a promise God had given her. She carried that bag full of pebbles as she journeyed with her companions, Sorrow and Suffering.

As they were walking along one day, a severe thunder and lightning storm came upon them. The only place they could find refuge was in a little cave, where they had to stoop down low to crawl into it. Just as they were safely secured inside, torrential rains fell and created a waterfall that cascaded over the opening to their cave, but not a drop of water touched them.

Still, Much-Afraid was despondent. She didn't know how they were going to get out of that cave. Reaching into her cloak, she pulled out the leather bag containing her "pebble promises" and dumped them all into her lap. She was so discouraged and dismayed that she wondered if she should just throw them away. "Were they not all worthless promises?" But instead of just tossing them all, she picked up the first one—and she remembered what the Good Shepherd had said to her when He had given it to her. "I will make thy feet like hinds' feet and set thee upon thine High Places" (Habakkuk 3:19 *KJV*). Then she picked up the next pebble and spoke the promise God had given her with that one. "What I do thou knowest not now; but thou shalt know hereafter" (John 13:7 *KJV*). One by one, Much-Afraid remembered God's promises that He made to her. By the time she had finished picking up all twelve pebbles and reciting their promises, her faith was rebuilt.

She put the stones back into her leather bag and hid them away, close to her heart. Later in the story, after Much-Afraid climbs to the mountaintop, the Chief Shepherd turns these pebbles into beautiful jewels and then places them in a royal crown for her to wear on her head.

In times of crisis, rehearse the promises of God. Those promises have the power to rebuild your faith and to change your thoughts, your attitude and your behavior. Read His promises over and over, and then mark them in your Bible in a way that is meaningful to you. I like to date these promises as God gives them to me. I also star them, underline them, and write them on note cards. Do whatever you need to do to get those promises from the pages of your Bible to your heart because that's where they're needed.

I cannot tell you how many times these words from Habakkuk have rushed back to me when I've needed them most—and often when I don't have a Bible nearby. I was driving to a conference with Gail Mays and Jean McClure one time, when out of nowhere, a big van came up behind us and pushed us off the road! That's all that happened, but it could have been so much worse. We could have flipped our car or tumbled off an embankment. But thankfully we didn't. It happened so fast that there wasn't time for us to react or do anything to help ourselves. But earlier I had been meditating on God's promise in Psalm 91 to give His angels charge over us. We had prayed before we left and asked God to protect us—and He did. We never found out why that van ran us off the road, but it didn't matter. God had shown Himself mighty on our behalf to keep us from getting hurt. And God wants to do miracles for you as well.

I've discovered that it's not the joyful circumstances that produce trust in God—it's the journey through the valleys and the impossible places. Just like with Much-Afraid, God is using every crisis, every difficulty in your life to build your trust in Him. He doesn't want you to remain as immature babes in your faith, always crying and never trusting.

One afternoon at one of our conferences I was in the lobby with Cheryl. I noticed a young mom holding her baby girl who wouldn't stop crying. So Cheryl, who is a wonderful mother—and now a grandmother—took the baby in her arms and rocked her, but that baby cried even harder. Well, I'm Grandma Kay, you know. I have nineteen grandchildren and over twenty great-grandchildren (and counting). So I took that baby and started rocking her. And she just cried all the more. I thought, *Oh, baby ... you can trust me. You can trust me.* What I really wanted was for that little baby to bond with me in three minutes and to love me and trust me with all her heart.

I think God lovingly cradles us like babies in His arms and says the same thing to each one of us. "Trust Me ... just trust Me."

But what's our reaction? "No, not You. I need my husband. I need my best friend. I need a self-help book." How horrible those words look when we put them out there like that. But isn't that essentially what we're saying when we turn to things and other people instead of turning to the Lord? How unwise that is, especially since God's Word promises that if we will put our trust in Him, and acknowledge Him in everything, He will direct our path (Proverbs 3:5-6).

When we are fully trusting God—really and truly trusting Him—we'll be able to rejoice. We won't rejoice over the problem, but we'll rejoice over the fact that God is God, and He is able to work all things for our good.

Habakkuk was called the perplexed prophet. And one of the things that perplexed him was why God would use an evil nation such as the Chaldeans to invade and chasten Israel for their wrongdoings. Habakkuk questioned a few things. He first questioned if God was even paying attention to him. "O LORD, how long shall I cry, and You will not hear?" (Habakkuk 1:2). This showed a definite lack of faith. At the very least, he denied the fact that God is always with us.

In verse 13 he questions why God seemingly does not care about what is happening.

> You are of purer eyes than to behold evil, and cannot look on wickedness. Why do You look on those who deal treacherously, and hold Your tongue when the wicked devours a person more righteous than he?

While he is waiting for God to answer his questions, he decides to go up to his watchtower.

> I will stand my watch and set myself on the rampart, and watch to see what He will say to me, and what I will answer when I am corrected (Habakkuk 2:1).

I love that. Habakkuk knew God was going to reprove him for his lack of trust. He was ready for it. Do you position yourself so God can speak to you? Are you willing to wait on Him? Or do you go your merry way and forget that God is in control? Position yourself. Pray. Ask Him, "Lord, what's going on here? What do You want to say to me? I'm going to place myself on this watchtower and I will wait for you."

In chapters 2 and 3, God answers Habakkuk by giving him a glorious revelation of who He is and what He was about to do.

> He stood and measured the earth; He looked and startled the nations. And the everlasting mountains were scattered, the

perpetual hills bowed. His ways are everlasting. You divided the earth with rivers. The mountains saw You and trembled … the sun and the moon stood still (Habakkuk 3:6; 9-11).

What a beautiful, poetic description of God's splendor and His power! We serve a sovereign, mighty, majestic God—a God big enough and powerful enough to create the stars, the moon, the earth, and everything upon it and above it—yet we don't trust Him to help us with our problems. He is such a glorious God and yet we're so weak in our faith. Learn to read the Word with an eye to see God's power and might and glory, and your problems will shrink right down in the light of His magnificence.

Finally, when Habakkuk had a vision of the awesomeness of God, he realized that the famine was nothing. It was nothing in comparison to the power of God. That's when he wrote these faith-filled words in chapter 3:

> Although the fig tree shall not blossom, neither shall fruit be in the vines; the labor of the olive shall fail, and the fields shall yield no grain; the flock shall be cut off from the fold, and there be no herd in the stalls …

This is a picture of famine. Maybe you're in a famine today, and you don't see any relief in sight. Remember that little three-letter word … "yet." "Although there's famine, *yet* I will rejoice in the Lord, I will joy in the God of my salvation."

Right now I want you to relinquish the deepest, most difficult problem you have, and I want you to express joy to the Lord—because He's in control and you can rejoice in Him. Are you willing to do that? Praise Him out loud. Speak a word of praise to the God you serve—the One who is capable of solving any problem. Say, "Thank You, Lord. I am trusting You to meet that 'although' for me."

> The LORD God is my strength, and He will make my feet like hinds' feet. And He will make me to walk on my high places (Habakkuk 3:19).

Hinds are female deer. I once read an interesting fact that the female deer has better footing than the male as she goes up the mountain. How we need that encouragement as pastors' wives! We can rest knowing that God will give us sure footing as we go up the hills of difficulty before us.

So many times when I've been in a place of great sadness, I've heard the Lord's promise: "Kay, I'm doing a work that you don't know about." We must remember His presence when the road gets steep or rocky, when life brings disappointments, or when your loved ones make choices that break your heart. We must determine not to allow fear to drive us, but instead to turn towards God and allow Him to lead the way.

Remember my grandson's wedding I mentioned at the beginning of this chapter? His bride was truly lovely. On that day, while she waited in the bride's room, Cheryl walked up to her and said, "Oh, you look so beautiful!"

She replied, "That's because I'm marrying the love of my life."

Isn't that precious? She didn't take the credit for herself. "The bride eyes not her garment, but her dear Bridegroom's face." [11]

I was so blessed by her love for him. And you know, from the very beginning of their relationship, if she was with us and someone suggested, "Hey, let's go do such and such," the first thing she did was look at him and see if he was okay with that suggestion. She got his "okay" or she got his "I'd rather you not," and either way, she just gazed at him with the most loving eyes. You know, she gazed. She loves her bridegroom, and all she wanted to know was what he'd like her to do.

That's a good picture for all of us to remember.

Chapter Eleven

AN ETERNAL PERSPECTIVE

ONE THING about living in Southern California is that every year we face the threat of wildfires. It's not quite a threat to our specific neighborhood, but we know many people who live in areas vulnerable to them. Many times we've had to pray for friends whose homes were in the line of a fire.

Once when Chuck was away our friend, Ralph, called.

"Is Chuck there?"

I could tell by his tone it was something urgent. "No, Chuck's not here. He's in Washington, DC," I said. "What's happening?"

All Ralph said was, "There's a fire. I can't talk … I've got to evacuate. I've got to evacuate!"

I immediately called some prayer warriors and asked them to spread the prayer request to everyone they knew. We prayed all night, and the next morning we learned that Ralph and his family had gotten out in time.

But his words stuck with me. I kept hearing, "I've got to evacuate!" At first, I thought about what it would be like if I had to evacuate my own house at a moment's notice. Then I started thinking about how glorious it will be when the Lord comes for us, and we have to evacuate the earth. What a wonderful, marvelous thought that is! I can hardly wait for that day.

But I want to ask you to think about this: If Jesus came for you right now, would you be ready to evacuate? Can you say you've faithfully done everything God has called you to do? It's a sobering thought. One of these days we're going to hear that evacuation cry and we're going to be home with Him. At that point, our opportunity to lay up treasures in heaven will be over—either we will have done it or not.

Now, some may argue with me, but I'm convinced there's no one on earth who is given more opportunities to serve God and to lay up treasures in heaven than a pastor's wife. We've been given an extraordinary privilege. Yet there are pastors' wives who don't like the ministry and don't see it as a privilege. This is the woman who doesn't want to bother laying up treasures in heaven. She's bored. Her attitude is, "I'm young. Why do I have to go to church every Sunday? Why do I have to live this way?"

I hope you've never had those thoughts. Sometimes, in order to hinder our ministry or rob us of a reward, the enemy works that kind of rebellion in our hearts and in our attitudes. We'll still do the work that's required of us, but we'll do it with resentment instead of for love's sake. And then instead of laying up treasure, which we can offer to the Lord when we see Him face to face, all we'll have to lay at His feet will be wood, hay and stubble. I believe the woman at risk of this is the one whose eyes are fixed firmly on this temporal life, and not on the eternal.

I once heard a teaching by Warren Weirsbe in which he declared, "We don't think often enough about heaven." I'm certain this is true. And that's surprising when you consider how wonderful heaven is. We'll have no more sorrow, or pain, or injuries, or emergency hospital trips, or heart-stopping phone calls in the middle of the night. No death. Instead, we'll dwell forever with God, blessed beyond anything we've experienced here on the earth.

And yet … we keep gazing at earth. We fill our lives with a lot of temporal activity. We collect too much temporal stuff and we fix our minds on a whole lot of temporal nonsense. And sometimes, because we've overloaded ourselves with nothing, the ministry gets lost in the clutter.

You know how that can be. You wake up to a long to-do list, having high hopes of accomplishing everything on it. Then comes that one phone call which interrupts the whole list. Somebody calls and says, "I'm divorcing my husband," and your internal reaction is, *Would you put that off for two weeks or so? Because I am busy every day between now and then.*

We can so easily see those phone calls as interruptions, but those phone calls are the ministry. Ministry doesn't present itself in a nice, orderly fashion. By the time those problems get to us, they've become life and death issues. At times, you feel like you're the very last person who should be handling that crisis.

We really are just clay pots, you know. We have no strength of our own; it all comes from God. If we empty ourselves of all the unimportant things, we make room for the Holy Spirit. And if our hearts are fixed on heaven, and not on earth, we can let His light shine through all the cracks and crevices in our lives and spill out onto those we're trying to minister to.

In 2 Corinthians 4:7-18, Paul encourages us about this.

> But we have this treasure in jars of clay to show that this all-surpassing power is from God and not from us. We are hard pressed on every side, but not crushed; perplexed, but not in despair; persecuted, but not abandoned; struck down, but not destroyed. We always carry around in our body the death of Jesus, so that the life of Jesus may also be revealed in our body. All this for your benefit, so that the grace that is reaching more and more people may cause thanksgiving to overflow to the glory of God. Therefore we do not lose heart. Though outwardly we are wasting away, yet inwardly we are being renewed day by day. For our light and momentary troubles are achieving for us an eternal glory that far outweighs them all. So we fix our eyes not on what is seen, but on what is unseen. For what is seen is temporary, but what is unseen is eternal (*NIV*).

Maybe you're feeling hard pressed on every side. That's a common experience in the ministry, because the needs come at us from all directions. As pastors' wives, we do suffer for the sake of our churches. We have many joyful experiences, but along with those, we also go through hard, perplexing, and difficult things—still, we do it for the sake of the Lord.

This passage is a wonderful reminder for us. Though we may feel weak, fragile, or unequipped, we can rest knowing that nothing we do in the ministry comes from our own strength. It's all the Lord. He does the work, and He works through clay pots in order that He gets the glory.

So don't lose heart. When we see that "outwardly we are wasting away," we rejoice, knowing that "inwardly we are being renewed day by day." I love that. This clay pot may be aging and wrinkling, but inwardly I'm being renewed. How I praise Him for that! I suggest you read this passage often and remember all the promises it contains. Remind yourself that no matter how hard your struggles are now, there's an eternal glory waiting for you which far outweighs all the difficulties.

Second Corinthians 4:18 gives us the secret to living life in such a way that we're ready to go at a moment's notice—with no regrets that we've left work undone here on earth.

> So we fix our eyes not on what is seen, but on what is unseen. For what is seen is temporal and what is unseen is eternal.

This is the heart of the issue for most of us. We are too transfixed by what is seen, and not captivated enough by what is unseen. It is like the old poem says:

> "The world is too much with us; late and soon,
> Getting and spending, we lay waste our powers:
> Little we see in Nature that is ours;
> We have given our hearts away, a sordid boon!" [12]

It really is a mystery to me how people can be so taken with this dark, wicked world and the things in it. Honestly, I can hardly bear it. I have become a complete misfit for this world. I don't like its laws. I don't like its customs. I don't like its values. My spirit is absolutely grieved by what I see all around me—by the blatant profaning of

God's name everywhere I look. There truly is nothing here that should consume the thoughts and attention of a woman of God. Yet so many Christian women *are* consumed with this world. As A.W. Tozer said, "The problem with most of us is the gaze of our soul is on this world." [13]

I once read a quote which summed it very well: "Stop living as though this life is all that matters." [14] We know the unbeliever lives this way. But did you realize we can be just as guilty? We can worry just as much about what to eat, what to drink, and what to wear as any other person. Instead, as women who belong to Jesus, we're told not to worry about those things. Jesus said,

> For your heavenly Father knows that you need all these things. But seek first the kingdom of God and His righteousness, and all these things shall be added to you (Matthew 6:32-33).

Charles F. Kettering said, "We should all be concerned about the future because we will have to live the rest of our lives there." [15] Isn't that interesting? God made us for an eternal purpose, but we've become too earthbound. We've become earth-*focused*. And this affects everything we do.

When we talk about perspective, we're really describing a person's viewpoint about what is important. Our perspective on the future determines our choices today. It's very easy to spot someone who believes that this life is all there is. You can see it in their choices. They look out for themselves, they live for pleasure and recreation, they accumulate as many toys as possible, and they don't care who's hurt in the process. These are people who jump from one relationship to another, because the minute things get hard or they feel a little bit unhappy, they run.

On the other hand, you can also tell when a person has an eternal perspective. They show by their values and priorities and lifestyle that their heart is in another place. Eternity is more real to them than earth, and they weigh everything in the light of heaven. While they are here, God is fashioning them for their eternal home. C.S. Lewis said, "Our character is a sum total of our responses to God's hidden working in our heart." When we're thinking on things eternal, we're much more prone to realize God's workings and promptings and to be obedient to them.

Chuck likes to say, "Don't be concerned with what you leave behind. But be concerned with what you'll send ahead." Weigh life's options on the scales of eternity. Ask yourself some challenging questions: What difference will that activity make in eternity? How much of what I'm spending my time on will God consider valuable in light of eternity? What am I giving my life to? Do my goals and values reflect what I believe?

Get alone with the Lord and ask Him, "By the way I've lived my life in Your presence, Lord, what do You think I'm living for?" Then ask a friend the same question. "By the way I live my life in your presence, what do you think I'm living for?" You might get some interesting answers.

"Let temporal things serve your use but the eternal be the object of your desire." [16] Don't you like that? We need to use a lot of temporal stuff, but the eternal should be our desire. Every object has a certain worth based on the illusion of durability and permanence. God determines something's value by its eternal significance. So with God, it is the eternal which counts the most.

Maybe for you it's not the allure of the world that gets your eyes off of heaven, but you're alarmed at the world and what you see in it.

Every day we see more and more evidence of the downward spiral of man, and it can so burden us that we forget to look up. I'm reminded of that portion of *Pilgrim's Progress* [17] where Christian and Hopeful approached the Delectable Mountains. (By the way, don't you just love the idea of Hopeful being your companion?) The place where they walked was simply beautiful—full of orchards and vineyards, gardens and fountains. There they met four shepherds named Knowledge, Experience, Watchful and Sincere. These shepherds invited them to have dinner with them and then to spend the night.

The next morning, as a warning to Christian and Hopeful, the four shepherds took them to several mountains where they viewed things that chilled them through and through. The shepherds wanted Christian and Hopeful to stay on the King's Highway—the holy way, the right path. What Christian and Hopeful saw shook them so badly, they lost sight of the celestial city.

I've experienced that myself. I've been so shaken at times by life's events that all of a sudden I've forgotten the most important things. I've forgotten Jesus is here. I've forgotten to put on the whole armor of God. I've forgotten to reach for the Word. Have you ever been in that place?

I think that's what happened to these two pilgrims as they were on their journey. But the wise shepherds knew that before Christian and Hopeful departed and continued on their journey, they needed a fresh perspective. So they took them up a hill called Clear and they handed them what they called a "perspective glass," which is something like a telescope. As each of them looked through it, they saw the one and only thing that mattered: the celestial city.

We read that Christian and Hopeful were still so shaken by all the calamity they had seen, that when they picked up the perspective glass, their hands shook so badly they barely made out the gate in the distance. But they did see that touch of glory. And you know what? It was enough to set their hearts afire, and they started back on the King's highway singing and rejoicing.

That's what happens when you look up from the calamity around and focus again on heaven. One glance at the Lord Jesus Christ can quicken your heart and change your perspective. Remember the song,

> "Turn your eyes upon Jesus,
> Look full in His wonderful face.
> And the things of earth
> Will grow strangely dim
> In the light of His glory and grace." [18]

Oh, how we need to turn our eyes on Him, and on heaven, and on the glories that await us there!

The eternal perspective is powerful and it can greatly change your life! Here's a short list of just a few of the things it can do for you.

AN ETERNAL PERSPECTIVE GIVES YOU A CALM HEART.

When we forget that we're only pilgrims passing through this life, we can easily get overwhelmed by a world in crisis. We can lose heart and peace of mind. But when we remember heaven, and we remind ourselves that God is still on the throne and that all things are working out according to His perfect plan, we can remain calm even in the midst of the worst calamity.

The Privilege

AN ETERNAL PERSPECTIVE GIVES YOU GRACE IN THE MIDST OF DISAPPOINTMENT.

It's so easy, when our eyes are fixated on this life, to let little things turn into big things. But when we're mindful of heaven, we can let molehills be molehills. We don't have to turn those little things into mountains.

Years ago we went to a convention in Keswick, England. It's a wonderful event mostly attended by evangelical Anglicans—many of whom are Oxford or Cambridge graduates. If ever there was a time in my life when I wanted to look right and behave myself, it was then.

I have very fine hair, but I have tons of it, and it has been a problem for me since I was a little girl with a Buster Brown haircut. So just before we went to England, I got a permanent. My hair looked great when we left the States, but there was a heat wave in England and it did something awful to my hair. It swelled up and just stuck out every which way. Nearly every woman I passed on the street had short, flat hair. And there I was with my wild and crazy hair. It was really horrible.

At mealtimes when we sat with all those Oxford and Cambridge graduates and their proper wives, I could just feel the unspoken thought in the room. I mean, some were very gracious to me, but I'm sure others were thinking, *Look at that crazy Californian.* You can get by with a lot if you're from California. Still, I was embarrassed.

One day I was walking by myself along a beautiful little river called Greta. I had just been to one of the church tent services where at least 2,000 people had heard a wonderful teaching and then we had a time of singing together. You can imagine how beautiful it is to hear 2,000 people worshipping all at once. So as I walked to the hotel, I was still worshipping the Lord. But then I remembered my hair, and I thought, *Lord, why do I feel so humiliated by this? I wish that my flesh were dead and I didn't feel this way.*

Then God spoke so lovingly to my heart. He said, "Kay, it doesn't matter to Me and it doesn't matter eternally." And you know what happened? From that moment on, my hair no longer bothered me. It didn't get any better, mind you—but it no longer affected me. Just that one reminder of eternity helped me to put my thoughts in perspective and get over my disappointment.

AN ETERNAL PERSPECTIVE SIMPLIFIES YOUR LIFE.

I don't know if you've noticed this, but most of us have a tendency to complicate and clutter our lives. We start out with one little cookbook, and before you know it we have twenty-five. Chuck was encouraging me to get rid of all my cookbooks. He said, "We eat the same thing most of the time anyhow." He's right. I don't even use those cookbooks! I could also throw out a bunch of the spices and herbs cluttering up my cupboard. Most of them I've never used and never plan to use. I don't know why I've kept them all this time … I think I just like the look of the bottles.

The closer we get to eternity, the more removed we should become from the world and its tinsel. This means less accumulating and collecting. It means giving things away, and holding things with an open hand. Whatever we have should belong to God and be at His disposal. If we're clutching and hoarding things, it shows our gaze is too set on this world. An eternal perspective doesn't lay up treasures on earth; it lays up treasures in heaven.

AN ETERNAL PERSPECTIVE CREATES CONTENTMENT.

I'm a little amazed when I look at my life now and I think back to when Chuck and I first got married. I was so fashion-conscious back then; however, I learned pretty quickly that I couldn't continue shopping like that. Chuck's salary didn't allow it, and it wasn't necessary in our congregation anyway. Do you realize that your church doesn't need you to wear the latest fashions? They want you to love them and reveal Christ to them and influence them toward God. We need to learn to be content with dressing modestly and simply. An eternal perspective teaches you this.

It helps you to embrace the thinking that "simplicity is enough." Instead of griping about the house you have, or the fact that the sheets and towels are a bit worn, or the dishes aren't real china, be satisfied with what God has given you. You'll remember that this is not your home, and that heaven is waiting for you—and it's going to be infinitely more beautiful than any home on earth.

I have to confess that there's one thing I cannot stand, and it's when I hear a pastor's wife complaining to her husband about his salary. It grieves my heart so badly, and I think it grieves Christ's heart too. It grieves Him when you are not happy living within your means.

I say that to you in love, and I say it understanding how hard it can be to adjust your expectations. I had to do it too. I was a real spoiled brat when we got married, because my dad had always given me money. I didn't know what it was like to go without, and I fully expected that Chuck would be like my daddy too. But God had some lessons for me to learn. He wanted to teach me to just trust Him and He would give me whatever I needed. I believe that through this issue of finances, God taught me more about faith in the first twenty years of our ministry than I ever learned through seeing healings or other miracles.

Be content with what you have. Don't gripe about your finances. Live without if you have to. You'll see what a blessing it can be.

AN ETERNAL PERSPECTIVE KEEPS YOU FROM SELF-OBSESSION.

I live in an area where women are expected to be ultra thin and without one wrinkle. So I know how easy it can be to worry about how we look. But the truth is, an eternal perspective keeps you from worrying about your weight. Now, it's good to have a proper respect for these things. It's good to want a healthy body so you're able to do any work the Lord wants to entrust to you. But we women tend to take those thoughts to the extreme. We become obsessed. God wants to free us from that. He wants us to rest in the knowledge that even with an extra ten pounds, our robes of righteousness will still fit. And once we reach heaven, we'll have new bodies waiting for us—perfect bodies. There's no sense in obsessing over this corrupt body now.

AN ETERNAL PERSPECTIVE MAKES YOUR RELATIONSHIPS BETTER.

When you're living in the light of eternity, conscious of that reality and aware of how soon it could arrive, you will react a lot differently when your husband squeezes the toothpaste tube in the middle. You will. You'll have more patience and more grace for him. I think perhaps the lack of an eternal perspective has been the ruin of more marriages than anything else. It's so easy to walk away … until you remind yourself that you're on the earth to serve the Lord, and He has asked you to serve and love and bless that man at your side.

When you're living life with an eye on heaven, you'll also parent differently. You won't look at parenting as something to be endured, but as an opportunity to plant eternal truths into the hearts of those children. What a blessed responsibility!

AN ETERNAL PERSPECTIVE KEEPS YOU PRESSING FORWARD.

The apostle Paul may not have lived in our fast-paced society, but he knew what it was to be hard pressed on every side, troubled and perplexed. In 2 Corinthians 1:8, describing their condition while in Asia, he said they were "pressed out of measure, above strength, insomuch that we despaired even of life" (*KJV*). This means they were pushed beyond the strength to endure. Have you ever felt that way? Maybe you feel that way today.

Despite it all—the constant pressure, the cares of all the churches, the beatings, the persecutions—Paul still penned these beautiful words in Philippians 3:13-14:

> But one thing I do, forgetting those things which are behind and reaching forward to those things which are ahead, I press toward the goal for the prize of the upward call of God in Christ Jesus.

To press in this way means to pursue steadfastly, earnestly, and with all the strength and diligence and determination within you. That's what we want to do as pastors' wives while we wait for the Lord. We want to continually reach forward, pressing toward the mark.

I once read about a woman who was mummified by the ashes in Pompeii when Mount Vesuvius erupted in AD 79. Since reading about her, I have been to Pompeii and I've actually seen her mummified remains. Her toes point toward the gate of escape, but her right arm is reaching back for something. It was discovered during the excavation of those remains that she was reaching back for a bag of pearls.

I wonder how many pastors' wives have lost their eternal perspective and they are reaching back toward a worthless bag of nothingness while destruction rages all about? We can't let it happen. Lives are at stake—

and God has chosen us to reach out to them and to minister to them. We must forget everything else except pressing toward God and toward eternity. It's not far off. Heaven is very near. You can't help but realize that when you look around at the world today and you see how far down sin is dragging people.

Not long ago, Chuck and I were invited to a big banquet meeting of CEOs. I was able to sit with a dear woman by the name of Sharon Newman, and we began talking about all the troubling world events that were currently in the news—wars, drive-by shootings, and all sorts of horrific crime. The more we talked about it, the more our shoulders drooped. Until Sharon turned and looked me straight in the eye. "You know," she said, "I think I hear the steps of the Bridegroom."

Both of us suddenly straightened right up. Joy flooded my soul and I was instantly aware of how close His return is. It won't be long now. We're at the gate of eternity. How exciting and glorious it will be when we step through!

While we wait, dear one, take care of every bit of business God has given you. Pray for those who need your prayers. Share Jesus with those who don't yet know Him. Love the ones God has entrusted to you. And be sure to feed your spirit far more than you feed your flesh. Whichever one you feed the most will be the one which takes control of your life—and dictates your perspective.

> "Face to face shall I behold Him
> Far beyond the starry sky
> Face to face in all His glory
> I shall see Him by and by!" [19]

Chapter Twelve

AS FOR ME

*I*N 1996, Cheryl and Brian, as well as our four grandchildren, moved to London to start a Calvary Chapel. Even though we knew God was calling them to go, it was still a very painful parting for all of us. Grandpa cried. Grandma cried. The kids sobbed. Cheryl and I just held each other … it was quite a scene.

Our granddaughter, Kelsey, who was seven at the time, had spent that last night with us. The next morning, as we were getting ready to leave for the airport, I was in our bedroom combing her hair and trying very hard not to think, *This is the last time I'll get to do this.* Kelsey turned around with sad eyes and said, "Grandma, if it wasn't the Lord's will, we wouldn't be going to London."

She was so precious, and I didn't want her to be sad. I said, "Oh, I know that, Honey."

As though I hadn't heard her the first time, she said it again. "If it wasn't the Lord's will, we wouldn't be going to London."

Again I said, "I know, Honey." By then her hair was combed and I sent her downstairs to be with Grandpa. A few minutes later I went to join them and saw Grandpa and Kelsey cuddled together in a chair. The tears were pouring down her face and there were some in Grandpa's eyes too. And I thought, *Come now, Lord. Take us all home. I can't bear this.*

Pretty soon it was time to leave. As we were walking out the door toward the car, Kelsey turned to me again and said, "Grandma …" Her little voice was wavering like it does when a child wants to cry. "If this wasn't God's will we wouldn't be going to London."

At this point I was trying very hard to keep from crying too. "Oh, I know, Honey."

Then she said it again. Chuck and I looked at each other, not knowing what else we could say to her. Then finally she looked up at me and said, "Grandma, why is it God's will?"

I thought, *I wish I knew … I wish I knew.* But I really did know. I knew her daddy was called to go. When they first told us they were leaving, I had asked Brian to tell me exactly what had happened to make him feel he was called to London. He said, "Kay, five weeks ago I was on my knees at five o'clock in the morning, and I was asking God to send someone to London. I kept praying, 'God, send someone to London.' Finally the Lord said, 'Why should I send someone else when I'm calling you?'"

Chuck and I first went to London in the early seventies, and then we went quite regularly. We've been all over England now, and Chuck has held two-week conferences there with the Keswick Conventions a number of times. But the very first time we went, I felt an intense burden for the country—especially for London. That burden just grew and grew with every visit to England. Chuck would be at one of the pastors' conferences with all the men, while I'd stay in our room and cry out to God for London, asking Him to send someone to reach them.

So when Cheryl and Brian told us what God was asking them to do, I said through tears, "I have prayed for England for so many years. I have yearned for their salvation … I just didn't know what the cost would be."

I want you to think about that. There's a cost to serving Jesus … and the cost will not just be to you, but also to those around you—to your parents, your children and your friends.

When I was a little girl, every Christmas my mom always made me give away one of my favorite dolls to the poor. I think she was afraid I wouldn't have a heart for poor people. But I have always had a heart for the poor, even though I really didn't want to give my doll away. But that was her requirement. And she wouldn't let me give just any doll. She wanted it to be a doll that I loved very, very much—usually my most favorite.

After Cheryl and Brian left, I was telling the girls at one of our pastors' wives' board meetings about what my mom used to do, and Sandy MacIntosh remarked, "God was training you then to give away one of your favorite dolls." I think she was right.

When we arrived at the airport and began to say our goodbyes, we were, of course, crying and hugging each other. Back then, you could walk people right up to the door of the plane. As Cheryl and the kids were sobbing and turning back for one last look at us, the ground attendant standing at the entry asked her, "How long will you be gone?" I'm sure she thought they were leaving forever by the way we were all carrying on.

Cheryl said, "Two years." They actually stayed nearly four, but we didn't know at the time it would be so long.

The attendant said, "Oh, that's hard, isn't it?"

Cheryl nodded.

Then the woman said, "I'll tell you what you need to do. When you get on the plane, get yourself a stiff drink."

That's the world's solution, isn't it? And then when that wears off, what do you do? You get another stiff drink, and then another. I stood watching them disappear through the door and I thought, *Oh, how grateful I am that my bundle of love that just got on the plane loves Jesus—all of them—and they've got a better solution by far.* And so have we. Amen?

I don't know what your preconceived idea was of being a pastor's wife. As I've told you, I married Chuck two months after we met, and three weeks later we took our first pastorate. I didn't have much time at all to think about my role. I simply waited on the Lord and did what seemed to come most naturally. I tried to be conscientious in my dress, and I loved the people. I still love them to this day. There was something so homespun and sweet about them. The whole thing was an experience and a joy. I can hardly remember anything that went wrong. I think that's a gift from God. It isn't that things didn't go wrong. They did. But there was something about being in the ministry and being a pastor's wife that I loved so deeply. I always have, and I still do.

The world is darker today than it was when I first became a pastor's wife. And because the days are getting worse, our job is getting heavier. We won't be able to fulfill the task the Lord has given us if we don't make a personal decision that says, "I am the Lord's, and nothing will sway me from serving Him."

When Joshua was near the end of his life, he gathered all the tribes of Israel at Shechem, and he began to recount the goodness of the Lord. He reminded them of how God called Abraham out of his pagan worship, and gave him Isaac. He reminded them when Israel was in bondage to the Egyptians, God delivered them out of bondage and opened the sea before them. And he spoke of all the victories God gave them—against the citizens of Jericho, against the Amorites, Perizzites, Canaanites, Hittites, Girgashites, Hivites and Jebusites.

As Joshua was impressing these reminders on their hearts, he looked out over the congregation and saw the intermingling they had allowed with the idols of the world. And I'm sure he was sickened in his spirit. When I see idolatry in our congregation, or when I hear of pastors' wives dabbling in the world and partaking in the ungodly behavior of the world, my heart is saddened and my spirit is sickened too.

Joshua knew that the children of Israel were intermingling with the world. He knew they had started living as the pagans lived. So he stood before them and issued a challenge:

Now therefore, fear the LORD, serve Him in sincerity and in truth, and put away the gods which your fathers served on the other side of the River and in Egypt. Serve the LORD! And if it seems evil to you to serve the LORD, choose for yourselves this day whom you will serve, whether the gods which your fathers served that were on the other side of the River, or the gods of the Amorites, in whose land you dwell. *But as for me and my house, we will serve the LORD* (Joshua 24:14-15, *emphasis added*).

After recounting all the goodness God had lavished upon the children of Israel, Joshua tells the people they need to make a decision. They need to decide whether they will serve the One true God, the God of their fathers, or the pagan gods of the surrounding people.

I issue the same challenge to you now. It's so easy to think that just because we're pastors' wives, we're fine. More than that, we can talk ourselves into thinking that we're wonderful because we're helping to lead a congregation. No, we're not wonderful. We're a bunch of ruined sinners. And just like the Israelites whom Joshua addressed, we face the same temptations to indulge in the pleasures of the world.

But the time to choose is now. We're either in His kingdom or we're in the kingdom of this world. Which will you choose? I am fed up with people living in the world and being part of the church, instead of living in God's kingdom and reaching out to a dying world. When we dabble with the world and its ways, our minds are polluted and our witness is diluted.

When Joshua stood and issued that challenge, he was speaking to *all* of Israel. He was talking to the leaders as well as to the people. You know, there's something very sobering about being a leader of the people. It's such a great and weighty privilege. You can be a leader who loves Jesus above all else and has made the decision to live completely unto Him, and walk your people toward heaven—or you can be a leader who wavers and leads people into confusion and darkness.

What I'm going to say may sound harsh, but it's my absolute conviction. I would rather that your church dwindle down to nothing than to continue with a pastor or a pastor's wife who doesn't want to serve God with a whole heart. If the gods of this world are enticing you, go serve them. Does that startle you? We're not used to that kind of straight talk, are we? But that's what Joshua said to God's people. And it needed to be said.

"Choose you this day whom you will serve" (Joshua 24:15). If you choose God, then love Him with all your heart. Serve Him with every ounce of strength. Live your life to His glory.

When the spies surveyed the land all those years before Joshua issued this challenge, only Joshua and Caleb came back with an encouraging report. They alone had faith that God would give them the land. That's because Joshua and Caleb were of another spirit. I love that. And I want you to be of another spirit. How can we be drawn to the junk of this world when we have the Holy Spirit—the very presence of God— dwelling within us?

Joshua beseeched the people to choose God over their idols, but he left the decision to them. "You do what you want to do," he said. "But as for me and my house, we will serve the Lord."

"As for me ..." It is a personal decision. No one can make it for you. You alone need to decide in which kingdom you will dwell. And as a pastor's wife, your decision will make an impact on all who are watching you.

When Paul wrote his first letter to Timothy, he encouraged him in his calling. He wrote,

> Don't let anyone look down on you because you are young, but set an example for the believers in speech, in life, in love, in faith and in purity. Until I come, devote yourself to the public reading of Scripture, to preaching and to teaching (1 Timothy 4:12-13 *NIV*).

Paul is talking to pastors, but whatever affects the pastor should also affect the pastor's wife, right? The essence of his message is this: Set an example for the believers. Set an example "in speech, in life, in love, in faith, in purity."

Do you want to know what the role is of the pastor's wife? There it is. That's it. You are to set an example for the believers. The very first thing Paul addresses in that verse is our speech. Don't pick up the world's vocabulary. I don't care what the words are or how common they become. Don't you use them. It isn't appropriate to your ministry. Be careful and watch your speech. As pastors' wives, we can set the church on fire by what we say.

If we're to set an example for the believers, we need to be mindful about what we *should* be saying as well. Initiate godly conversation with others. Talk about Jesus in your speech. Most times we're just so negligent. We talk about fashion. We talk about weight. We talk about wrinkles. We talk about all kinds of insignificant stuff. But we forget to talk about the One we love the most. We neglect to talk about Jesus. Our world is in such a mess and people need to hear how much our Savior loves them. We need a fresh touch on our lips, our tongues, our minds, our hearts—and we need boldness to share the gospel. Make your voice heard in this land.

Be an example of the believer in your lifestyle. Does the congregation know that you spend time with the Lord? I mean, you don't say, "I spent six hours today with Jesus." Nobody's impressed by that. But is there something fragrant and lovely coming forth from your life because you're spending time at the feet of Jesus? Are you spending that time with Him so that your lifestyle affects others?

Be an example of the Lord in love. If a stranger were to observe your life, would they conclude that you are a loving person? It's so easy to be cross or out of sorts when things don't go our way. For some of us, it's much harder to be gentle, patient and loving. Yet what did Jesus say would be the sign that we belong to Him? It would be love. He said, "By this all will know that you are My disciples, if you have love for one another" (John 13:35).

As a pastor's wife, you have so many opportunities to pour out love to people who come to you with so many different needs. We minister to those who are disgruntled, disheartened, disillusioned, sick, lonely, hurting, weary, worldly, wounded, angry, bitter, confused, frightened, insecure, burdened, cranky, crabby, critical, and troubled. Have you met any of those people? And those are just a few. There are also wonderful people who love to pray with us and read the Word together and share sweet fellowship. Be an example to all of them—the wounded ones and the wonderful ones.

Do you know how much it blesses the heart of God when you pull someone closer to Jesus through a touch or a prayer or a phone call? The flesh will resist. The flesh always resists the loving act. But if we spend time with Jesus, He'll cause the flesh to evaporate. He will empower us to love as we ought and to minister as the people need.

Do you want to be empowered in this way? I do. I want God's power flowing through my life in such a way that if I lay my hand on your shoulder in prayer, you're on fire for the Lord Jesus Christ. Don't you want that in your church? Wouldn't you like to be so filled with God's power that whenever you walk into your church, women suddenly encounter God? They might be whispering and chatting together, but when you walk in, Jesus Christ is made manifest to them. Listen, you cannot do it unless you have daily communion with Him. I know.

I've walked both ways. I got by as a Christian. I got by in the church okay and you are able to "get by" in the ministry as well. You can call on people and pray with them and counsel them and even teach a Bible study, but there won't be power in what you do unless you draw it from God. You won't have the power that changes other people's lives for eternity. I want that in my life and I want it for you. What a high privilege you've been given! To think that God's people would turn to you in their darkest hours—I am still so awed that He has entrusted His lambs to me. And how precious it is when you know you've made a difference in someone's life.

I remember once when a woman called me and said, "I feel like there's nothing worth living for."

God gave me His love for her. I said, "Oh, you are so darling. How could you possibly feel that way?" Then I told her, "You've brought joy to every group of people you've ever been a part of—I've seen it." I kept talking to her and loving her. I wanted her to focus on Jesus. So I said, "You know, you're here for one reason."

We're all here for one reason—and that's to minister to others. We're here to bless and minister to the Lord. We're here to minister to our husbands. Do you understand that? You're here to minister to him, not to demand that he be a perfect partner to you. If we all had a perfect marriage, who would need Jesus? He leaves empty spaces in our lives so that He can fill them. Sometimes your marriage is the thing that drives you closer to the Lord. But you commit that you're going to love him and bless him and minister to him in any way the Lord asks of you.

We're here to minister to our children and to lead them to Jesus. We're here to minister to the congregation and to anyone else God brings along our path.

I reminded this woman about all of that. And at the end of the call she said, "Why, when I talk to you, do I feel so much better?" Now, I'm just a wretched sinner just like you are, and I know it was only the Spirit of God working in me that allowed any fruit to come of that conversation. But it made me so joyful to know God used me. I do not feel worthy to be in the ministry, but He has allowed it. He has called me—and He has called you—to tend to His lambs.

Love your people. Minister to them. Take time for them. And you will be repaid a thousandfold. They will repay you by loving you back. If you walked through my house, I could point out all the sweet gifts people have given me over the years—just little tokens of love. It is so precious how God uses you to minister to others. And then He returns so much more than you could ever give.

One morning, not long after Cheryl, Brian and the kids had moved to London, I was in Chuck's office very early. I was still in so much pain missing them all horribly, but I wanted God's will to matter more to me. I needed to process all those feelings and I was trying hard to work through it. All of a sudden I raised my hands and reached out toward the Lord. Like David who said, "LORD, I have stretched out my hands to You" (Psalm 88:9), I stretched my hands out to Him and said, "Lord,

I need comfort. I need Your comfort." Then I started reading my Bible and I prayed for God to speak to me, asking Him to comfort me.

Then, for some reason, I looked up from my Bible and glanced around the room. There on the coffee table next to me was a little framed Scripture written in calligraphy, "For I know the thoughts that I think toward you, says the LORD, thoughts of peace and not of evil, to give you a future and a hope" (Jeremiah 29:11). Picking it up, I thought, *I didn't know I put that there. Where did I get this?* I turned it over, and I read what was written on the back. It had been given to me after I spoke at a Christmas luncheon … at Calvary Chapel Vista, Cheryl and Brian's church. It was a gift from Cheryl.

Can you imagine what that did to my heart? I felt as though she had spoken to me from the Word of God. I was breathless before the Lord. Oh, He is beautiful beyond description! "You know my sitting down and my rising up; You understand my thought afar off" (Psalm 139:2). And when we most need a touch of encouragement, He knows that too.

Cheryl had her own moments there in England. She was missing home as much as we were missing her. Of course, I never knew when she was struggling. But God knew. He saw. And just like He was doing for me at home, He brought her the comfort she needed in her darkest moments.

One morning when I was home alone, I found a piece of paper on which Chuck had scrawled a long series of numbers. The kids had only been gone a short time, and I hadn't yet seen a phone number for them in London … but I thought, *What if?* So I just picked up the phone and dialed those numbers.

"Hello?" I heard on the other end. It was Cheryl.

"Cheryl!" I said. Oh, I was so happy to hear her voice.

She started crying. "Mom, I was missing you so much and having such a hard time, that literally—just the moment before you called—I prayed and said, 'Lord, You know my every need. Right now, I just feel like I need to talk to my mom.' And the moment I said that, the phone rang. And here you are!"

We talked about the move and how everyone was adjusting to London, and then I was able to share with her some of what the Lord had been teaching me. I said, "Cheryl, I would never choose this pain for myself. I miss you so much. But I have found that when I'm in the most pain, the Lord draws closest to me. And through all of this, He's given me a depth of understanding and insight into His Word that I could have gotten no other way."

Oh, how good God is to meet us in that lonely place and to draw beauty out of our pain! As the psalmist said, "Give thanks to the LORD, for He is good!" (Psalm 136:1).

Years ago we had a day of fasting and prayer for the support leaders who serve in our Joyful Life ministry. We had such a beautiful time of prayer together, praying in English and praying in the Spirit, and just loving Jesus and asking Him for direction and guidance. Then I decided to read that verse from Psalm 136. "Oh give thanks to the LORD, for He is good."

You know, we hardly have any concept at all of the word "good" as it pertains to God. That's because we use that word in so many lesser ways. We say that someone is a good friend, or that the dinner was pretty good. But that doesn't come close to the way the word applies to God. So in this prayer time, I asked the women to share Scriptures they knew that spoke on God's goodness. For the next fifteen minutes or so, we shared from memory all the beautiful descriptions the Word gives us of the goodness of God. It was such a precious time of worship, and afterward several of the ladies told me they had never meditated on the word "good" as it pertains to God.

Have you? If not, I suggest you read a concordance and trace all the references which describe God's goodness. Then transfer the awe and wonder you gain straight to your people. Let them know how truly good and magnificent their God is. Oh, let your faith be known to your people! As pastors' wives, we must know our God. We must.

When Joshua stood before the people, he was able to declare, "As for me …" because he knew God. Let me ask you this: How many new things have you discovered about God this week? How about in the last few months? This is an easy test to take. Just sit down and begin listing all the new revelations you've received. Or maybe you want to begin listing everything you know about Him. Most people can say only five or ten things. That's it. That's all they know about God.

And yet, we have His inspired Word which reveals an astounding list of attributes describing God's nature and personality. He is loving, eternal, patient, just, longsuffering, forgiving, omniscient, sovereign, merciful, kind and compassionate … Oh, do you know our magnificent God? Do you know Him as well as you should? You can't stand before a congregation of people and say, "As for me …" unless you truly know God.

I want to know Him more and more and I'm constantly discovering new facets of His character. I could meditate for a month straight just on the fact that He's my high tower. Somebody asked me once during an especially trying time, "Kay, how can you stay so calm in these stresses?"

I said, "The worse they get, the quicker I go to 'the secret place of the Most High and dwell under the shadow of the Almighty.' He hides me in His secret pavilion and He just keeps me there. The storms rage, but I'm hidden away with Him."

Do you know what it's like to be in the shelter of God's presence? When somebody in your church pops off or does something cruel to you, do you let the Lord hold you in the palm of His hand? That's what you must do, beloved. Do not go to that person and try to set them straight. Do not go to ten other people looking for sympathy. Go to the Lord— that secret place of refuge. Hide away with your Lord and receive the comfort of His arms. Experience His mercy and His grace. And when you come out of that place, you are able to go back to the congregation in love, in faith, in purity and in strength. We need that strength when we've been hurt or when we're facing something painful and hard.

Cheryl and I had gone together to Calvary Chapel San Jose to speak to their women just before I found out that she and Brian were leaving. She hadn't said anything, but I could tell something was wrong, because she wasn't being herself. While she was teaching, I kept watching her and listening, and the more I did, the more worried I became. I said to the woman sitting next to me, "Something's wrong with Cheryl. What's wrong?" I was trying to nod my head in all the right places as she spoke, but I was so antsy I could hardly pay attention.

When the retreat ended, we flew back to Santa Ana together. On the flight home we talked about prayer needs for friends, and we talked about the teaching sessions—but we didn't touch on anything which accounted for the strain I could see in her. I really believed something was wrong, but I hoped she was just tired.

When we got home, Chuck was sitting at the kitchen table with his head down. He looked so sad and serious that I realized something was really wrong. Just as I was asking, "What is it? What's wrong?" Brian arrived, looking serious too.

We all sat down at the table with Chuck, who looked at me and said, "Did Cheryl tell you?"

"Tell me what?"

Brian, Cheryl and Chuck were all looking at each other, and then Chuck just put his head down again and said, "The kids are moving to London."

I shrieked.

Cheryl started crying. "Mom," she said, "I just want to do God's will."

I wish I could tell you that I nodded at that and said, "Oh. Well, then, that's what we must do, darling." Instead, I wailed. I sat there and I shrieked and sobbed and carried on like my heart had just broken in two.

It wasn't until the next morning that I was able to call and say what I most needed to say—what I truly wanted to say. Still, I said it between sobs. "Cheryl, I know this is God's will. I know you want to do His will. And that's what I want too." It was true in that moment, and it's true now. I want God's will. Because, you see, as for me and my house, we will serve the Lord.

I had questions, and lots of tears and pain. There was a lot of confusion that next morning, because this all coincided with a bit of drama we had going on with a deranged woman at church who was stalking Chuck. About two weeks earlier, a notebook was found in the church in which she had written a note to Chuck. She wrote, "You are sleeping with the devil. She tricked you into marriage, and Chuck Jr. is the result of that, and your wife and Chuck Jr. have no joy. He's all her seed, none of yours. And as soon as you get rid of this bondage, that Calvary machine will die and we can make you famous in the world."

The person who found the notebook brought it to me and I took it straight to Chuck. He wrote her a letter in return telling her not to come back to our church. Well, as it happened, she received Chuck's letter the same Saturday I discovered Cheryl was going to London.

So Sunday morning, I went to the church office just before second service and heard that Chuck had announced in the previous service, "I'm going through the greatest tragedy in my life." He couldn't explain any further because Brian hadn't yet told his church in Vista. So when I walked into church, everyone started looking at me with that "Oh, you poor thing" look.

I thought, *What's happening?* Well, right about then, I looked up at the closed-circuit TV in the office, and I saw the camera pan in on the deranged woman, who was standing in the sanctuary with her arms raised. I was staring at the crazy woman, and everyone else was staring at me with those looks of pity, and I thought something tragic must have happened concerning her.

They did end up taking her away in handcuffs later that day. But God always brings something good out of these awful circumstances. In the letter Chuck wrote to that woman, he said, "I married my wife because

I love her deeply, and my love has grown even more and more—and I am devoted to her." It was worth it just for the letter, let me tell you.

That same day, we went to lunch with Chuck Jr. and found out he had a stalker as well—and his stalker was even worse than the woman who had been after Chuck. It was really frightening. And all of this happened within a twenty-four-hour period. We have crazy days like that in the ministry. But, "As for me and my house, we will serve the Lord."

We have to remember this. We have to. We must keep this commitment firmly planted in our minds, because we do not know what the next day will bring or if the next phone call might shake our world.

The week that all of this tragedy was happening, I had actually scheduled a day to cry. Doesn't that sound funny? But I thought, *I need one day where I can just cry and get it all out.* So I planned on Tuesday for my cry day. Chuck was up in Seattle for a pastors' conference, so I would have the whole day to sit before the Lord and deal with my grief. But it wasn't to be. Tuesday morning, I received a call with news that a sweet friend of mine had attempted to take her life.

Immediately I went to the hospital, but I had to go through a bunch of locked wards before I found my friend. It was really frightening. I had my Bible, my purse and a little devotional book I wanted to leave with her. According to a guard who noticed my purse as I was leaving after my visit, they were supposed to have confiscated that. Isn't God good to let the Bible through? But as I was walking through the second locked door, I noticed a big warning sign. For a split second, I really didn't want to go through the door. Then the Lord reminded me, "You've got the sword of the Spirit with you. What else do you need?" It's such a comfort to have your Bible with you. That calmed me down. I was able to spend two-and-a-half hours talking and praying with my friend. I was so glad to see her and to have that time with her.

But that wasn't the end of my day. Not long after I got home from the hospital, I received a call from one of our pastors in Colorado. He had horrible news. Three boys had been murdered, and two of them were from his church. Two of the boys had come from California to help him construct the church building.

The pastor and his wife, Jeb and Chris, had taken in a boy from juvenile hall. Jeb said he'd been a sweet, gentle, tender kid during the time he was with them. But a few weeks before the murders, he moved out of their house and apparently started using crystal meth. When his girlfriend broke up with him, he went berserk. First he went to Jeb and Chris's house and killed the three boys who were living there. Then he stole a car and drove to the university where his ex-girlfriend was staying and held her and three other girls hostage. He kept telling her, "I'm going to kill you. You've taken my life. I'm going to take yours." At one point, he shot her in the foot. Finally, a sniper shot him when he put his head out the window.

Chuck came home the day after I got the phone call and we spent all night in prayer for Jeb and Chris and everyone involved. We were just so overcome with sorrow.

I waited another day before I called Chris. I knew the media was hounding her and her phone was ringing off the hook. To my knowledge, we had never met before, but we had the dearest conversation. She could have asked why, but she didn't. She could have said, "We took this boy in because we wanted to do the Lord's work. But now the whole world is going to think we're fools." But Chris didn't say any of that. Instead she said, "Kay, God is going to bring good out of this. I know He is."

The Privilege

This is a woman who knows Jesus. Her trust is in God, and she has chosen to stand steadfastly in her faith regardless of what may come. "As for me and my house, we will serve the Lord."

When you make that declaration, you are making a commitment. After commitment comes consecration. Do you know what that means? It means that you are wholly reserved for God's use, and God's use alone—just as the temple vessels, which were wrapped and carried in a special way, were used solely for the Lord. You belong to Him, and He can use your life in any way He desires. Are you consecrated to Him? It's so easy to glibly say, "Well, as for me and my house, we will serve the Lord." It rolls so nicely off the tongue. But are you living for God's use alone?

There's no more meaningful way to live your life than in dedicated service to the Lord. Ministers of Jesus Christ should never allow themselves to intermingle with the world—picking up its pleasures, diversions or its entertainment. We must live as close to the kingdom as possible. We must be asking, "Lord, is this Your will? Is this what You want me to do? Is this where You want me to be? Is this what You want me to be putting in front of my eyes?"

My prayer for you is that you will choose to be a consecrated woman. The time is short and the fields are white for harvest, and we can't afford to spend our lives on things that have no eternal value. I believe in rest and having fun and taking vacations—I do. But if we don't live lives that count for eternity, certainly our people won't either.

I want to continue growing until the day the Lord takes me home. I want to be changed daily. I want to live in such a way that the people He has entrusted to me can take hope from my example and find peace. They need for me to do that. They don't have the advantages I do. They don't live with the pastor. So my calling is to live in such a way that they benefit from my consecration.

What does a consecrated life look like? It looks different. It's different in all the ways that matter. There's a purity to your life. You don't wear suggestive clothing, you don't flirt, you don't give other men one single look that lasts longer than it should. Your speech is sanctified. You don't slip into swearing, as so many others do. You watch your language. You don't gossip. And when trials and tragedies come, you trust God and you share that faith with the ones who are watching you.

One day, back when I was still grieving over Cheryl, Brian and the kids leaving, I sat before the Lord reading my Bible and trying to work through all my feelings, when my heart heard Jesus say, "This is a cross in your life. This is a sacrifice."

When that word "sacrifice" came to mind, I thought, *How do any of our trials compare to what Jesus did for us?* I've never felt that I've really sacrificed—not really. We've gone without money, we've had terrible sorrows. We lost our parents by the time we were thirty-five. We've had all kinds of hard things happen in ministry. But I never did consider them big sacrifices—or sacrifices of any kind ... because God always pours in more than I could ever give up or give out.

So when the Spirit of the Lord met me in that moment and whispered that word to me, I stopped and said out loud, "Lord, do You really see this as a sacrifice?" The thought that I could sacrifice something for Him was breathtaking to me. I felt His Spirit say to my heart, "Yes, Kay. And it is fragrant unto Me."

Oh, how I long for my life to be a continual fragrance unto Him. I want to remain on the altar of sacrifice, where Kay is consumed and

Jesus remains. I want to be a sweet-smelling savor to the Lord. I hope you do too.

That last morning in our house, when Kelsey was so sad and teary, I remember looking for a way to cheer her up a little. So I said, "Let's say goodbye to the teddy bears." I have two teddy bears in the entry hall. I said, "They're going to sit there until you get back, Honey."

It didn't really help. The tears kept flowing, and she kept saying that same line to us—"If it wasn't the Lord's will, we wouldn't be going to London"—and I kept trying to think of some way to lessen her sadness. Finally, when we were in the car and heading for the airport, she started sobbing. "London's an ugly place," she said. "It's barren and it's dirty and I don't want to go there."

I thought, *All right, Lord. I need help—quickly.* And something came to me. I said, "Oh, Kelsey, it's not barren and dirty. It's beautiful. I looked it up in a book, and do you know what I found out? A king used to live near the place where you're going to live."

Her tears stopped then. Kelsey straightened up and said, "A king?" Just the thought of being near the place where a king lived changed her whole focus.

How about you? Do you realize you're going to live with the King one day? I hope that truth is alive to you today. I hope that when life brings you difficult moments, you let the promise of heaven carry you through. Are you, like Abraham, looking for that city? Are you a pilgrim and a stranger so focused on eternity that this world cannot glue itself to you in any way? Oh, are you ready to see the King?

He's coming soon, beloved. Make sure you are ready.

Oh, Father, our hearts hear the footsteps of the Bridegroom, and how we long for His return! We want to be a bride prepared. So we ask You, Lord, to do whatever You must to wake us up. Turn our gaze from the visible to the eternal. Do a work in us that we could never do ourselves—carve Your will onto our hearts and minds.

If ever the church needed pastors' wives who walk in love and talk in love and live in such a way that love flows freely from us to all we encounter … that time is now. So Jesus, would You teach us how to love as You love? Would You cause in us a devotion so strong and so determined that Satan is unable to touch us in thought or word or deed; unable to make us doubt You or Your purposes for us?

We know that it delights You when we put our trust fully in You, Jesus. So as our Good Shepherd, we just want to say that we trust You to lead us where You want us to go. We yield ourselves to You, Lord. May we live for Your glory alone.

We ask it in the most beautiful name we know … the name of Jesus.

Amen.

Footnotes

Introduction

[1] Hannah Hurnard, *Hinds' Feet on High Places*, (Carol Stream, IL: Tyndale House Publishers, Inc., 1975).

Chapter 1

[2] "Spiritual" Merriam-Webster Online. 18 August 2010 <http://www.Merriam-webster.com/dictionary/spiritual.

[3] William Cowper, "Exhortation to Prayer," 1779.

Chapter 2

[4] http://thinkexist.com/quotation/you_can_do_more_than_pray_after_you_have_prayed/ 159225.html.

Chapter 5

[5] Gayle Erwin, *The Jesus Style*, (Cathedral City, CA: Yahshua Publishing, 2002).

[6] ibid.

[7] Thomas O. Chisholm, "Living for Jesus," 1917.

Chapter 6

[8] James Rowe, "I Would Be Like Jesus," 1911.

[9] "Snow White and the Seven Dwarfs," Animated Film, Hollywood, CA: The Walt Disney Company, 1937.

Chapter 10

[10] ibid, Hurnard.

[11] Anne Ross Cundell, "The Sands of Time Are Sinking," 1876.

Chapter 11

[12] William Wordsworth, "The World Is Too Much With Us," 1807.

[13] A.W. Tozer, *The Pursuit of God*, (Harrisburg, PA: Christian Publications, 1982).

[14] Stacy Rinehart, Paula Rinehart, *Living for What Really Matters: Long-Term Values in a Short-Term World*, (Colorado Springs, CO: Navpress, 1986).

[15] http://www.inspirationalquotes4u.com/ketteringquotes/index.html

[16] Thomas á Kempis, quoted by Randy Alcorn, *Money, Possessions and Eternity.*

[17] John Bunyan, *Pilgrim's Progress*, (New York, NY: Oxford University Press: 1984).

[18] Helen Lemmel, "Turn Your Eyes Upon Jesus," 1922.

[19] Mrs. Frank A. Breck, "Face to Face," 1898.

Pleasing God
Book & Journal

In *Pleasing God,* Kay Smith exhorts and encourages women to think of God first and to live with His pleasure uppermost in mind.

Journal contains study questions for each chapter.

ISBN: 9781597510875

Reflecting God
Book & Journal

Further the journey that began in, *Pleasing God*, as Kay teaches the godly attributes necessary to reflect the very image of God.

Journal contains study questions for each chapter.

ISBN: 9781597510950

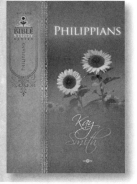

Philippians

If this world has robbed you of joy, learn to recover it through the secrets found in the book of Philippians, an in-depth Bible study taught by Kay Smith.

ISBN: 9781597510806

AUDIO RESOURCES BY KAY SMITH

PLEASING GOD MP3

Complete audio study of the Pleasing
God Bible study. Includes
questions for each message.
ISBN: 9781931713788

ATTRIBUTES OF A GODLY WOMAN MP3

A Bible study from the book of Titus,
teaching godly attributes to be passed to
the next generation. Includes questions
for each message.
ISBN: 9781931713733

BEHOLD THE HANDMAID OF THE LORD CD SET

Kay Smith shares fun and thought-
provoking messages surrounding the
ministry of a pastor's wife.
ISBN: 9781932941630

Leadership Resource

DWELLING IN THE HOLY OF HOLIES MP3

Kay Smith teaches women how to
draw close to the Lord through personal devotion. Includes study guide.
ISBN: 9781931713757

FOLLOWING HIS STEPS MP3

Includes 12 messages of Kay Smith
sharing with pastors' wives to follow
the footsteps of Jesus.
ISBN: 9781932941821

Leadership Resource

ORDERING INFORMATION:
THE WORD FOR TODAY
(800) 272-9673
www.twft.com • info@twft.com